cakes
& slices

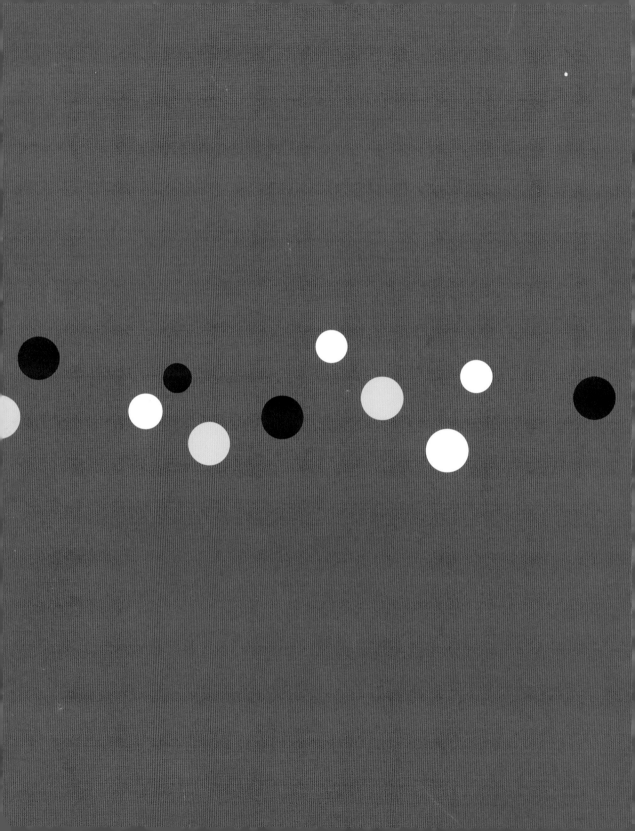

cakes & slices

MURDOCH BOOKS

contents

the sweet life

In a world gone mad with 'fast speed' this and 'instant' that, there's something deliciously therapeutic about donning an apron, rolling up your sleeves and getting into the kitchen to bake. It's just not a process that can be hurried; a cake needs slow, careful attention paid to the various stages involved, as do yummy slices with their chewy, gooey, crispy layers, iced tops or otherwise sugary finishes. Sure you can buy packet mixes, but their cheat's way to instant gratification comes at the expense of the incomparable flavour and mouth-melting texture of the real, homemade thing.

Thanks to electric beaters and cake mixers, much of the hard work has been removed from home baking. All you really need do is pay attention to a few simple rules such as, for example, preheating your oven, greasing or lining tins thoroughly, using softened butter for creaming, and always whisking egg whites using scrupulously clean bowls and beaters. Simple! The hardest part is determining what to whip up. Will it be a lemon ricotta slice … or a light-as-air sponge, oozing with jam and cream? Does the mood call for chocolate and, if so, in what guise? A decadent mud cake, maybe?

Using the tempting recipes in this book you'll be able to conjure fabulous home-baked treats suited to any occasion, from the poshest afternoon tea or a dinner-party dessert to casual, rustic sweet snacks suited to lunchboxes and mid-morning pick-me-ups.

light

Angel food cake with chocolate sauce

125 g (4½ oz/1 cup) plain (all-purpose) flour
230 g (8 oz/1 cup) caster (superfine) sugar
10 egg whites, at room temperature
1 teaspoon cream of tartar
½ teaspoon natural vanilla extract
silver cachous (balls), to decorate (optional)

Chocolate sauce
250 g (9 oz) dark chocolate, chopped
185 ml (6 fl oz/¾ cup) pouring (whipping) cream
50 g (1¾ oz) unsalted butter, chopped

Preheat the oven to 180°C (350°F/Gas 4). Have an ungreased angel cake tin ready. Sift the flour and 115 g (4 oz/½ cup) of the sugar into a large bowl, then repeat the sifting another three times. Set aside.

Beat the egg whites, cream of tartar and ¼ teaspoon salt in a bowl using electric beaters until soft peaks form. Gradually add the remaining sugar and beat until thick and glossy. Add the vanilla extract. Sift half the flour and sugar mixture over the meringue and fold into the mixture. Repeat with the remaining flour and sugar.

Spoon into the cake tin and bake for 45 minutes, or until a skewer inserted into the centre of the cake comes out clean. Gently loosen around the side of the cake with a spatula, then turn out onto a wire rack to cool completely.

To make the sauce, heat the chocolate, cream and butter in a saucepan over low heat, stirring, until smooth. Drizzle over the cake. Sprinkle with cachous, if desired.

SERVES 8

Butterfly cupcakes

120 g (4 oz) unsalted butter, softened
170 g (6 oz/¾ cup) caster (superfine) sugar
185 g (6½ oz/1½ cups) self-raising flour
125 ml (4 fl oz/½ cup) milk
2 eggs, at room temperature
125 ml (4 fl oz/½ cup) whipped cream
1½ tablespoons strawberry jam
icing (confectioners') sugar, to dust

Preheat the oven to 180°C (350°F/Gas 4). Line a 12-hole standard muffin tin with paper cases.

Beat the butter, sugar, flour, milk and eggs using electric beaters on low speed. Increase the speed and beat until smooth and pale. Divide evenly between the muffin holes and bake for 30 minutes, or until golden. Transfer to a wire rack to cool completely.

Cut shallow rounds from the centre of each cake using the point of a sharp knife, then cut in half. Spoon 2 teaspoons cream into each cavity. Top with 1 teaspoon of jam and position two halves of the cake tops in the jam to resemble butterfly wings. Dust with icing sugar.

MAKES 12

Berry and apple slice

150 g (5½ oz) unsalted butter
310 g (11 oz/1⅓ cups) caster (superfine) sugar
2 eggs, at room temperature, lightly beaten
250 g (9 oz/2 cups) self-raising flour, sifted
170 ml (5½ fl oz/⅔ cup) buttermilk
1 teaspoon natural vanilla extract
2 large apples
150 g (5½ oz/1 cup) blueberries
150 g (5½ oz/1¼ cups) blackberries
icing (confectioners') sugar, to dust

Preheat the oven to 180°C (350°F/Gas 4). Lightly grease a 20 x 30 cm (8 x 12 inch) rectangular shallow tin and line the base with baking paper, leaving the paper hanging over on the two long sides.

Beat the butter and sugar using electric beaters until light and fluffy. Add the egg gradually, beating well after each addition. Stir in the flour and buttermilk alternately and mix until smooth. Stir through the vanilla. Spread a 5 mm (¼ inch) layer of mixture over the base of the prepared tin.

Peel, quarter and core the apples. Cut into very thin slices and arrange on top of the mixture. Spoon the remaining mixture over the apple and smooth the surface. Scatter with the blueberries and blackberries. Bake on the middle rack of the oven for 40 minutes, or until cooked and golden.

Leave in the tin for 30 minutes, then lift out onto a wire rack to cool completely. Dust with icing sugar and cut into squares.

MAKES 12 PIECES

Sponge sandwich with jam and cream

4 eggs, at room temperature
1 teaspoon natural vanilla extract
115 g (4 oz/½ cup) caster (superfine) sugar
60 g (2¼ oz/½ cup) self-raising flour
60 g (2¼ oz/½ cup) cornflour (cornstarch)
2 tablespoons raspberry jam
310 ml (10¾ fl oz/1¼ cups) pouring (whipping) cream
icing (confectioners') sugar, to dust
coloured cachous (balls), to decorate (optional)

Preheat the oven to 180°C (350°F/Gas 4). Lightly grease two 20 cm (8 inch) round cake tins and line the bases with baking paper.

Beat the eggs, vanilla and sugar using electric beaters for 5 minutes, or until pale and creamy.

Sift the flours together on a sheet of baking paper. Gently tip the flour into the egg and sugar mixture and fold quickly and lightly using a large metal spoon — do not overmix. Divide the mixture evenly between the tins. Bake for 20 minutes, or until a skewer inserted into the centre of the cake comes out clean. Leave in the tins for 5 minutes, then turn out onto a wire rack to cool completely.

Spread one cake with the raspberry jam and whipped cream, then place the other cake on top. Dust with icing sugar to serve, and if desired, decorate with coloured cachous.

SERVES 8

Pear upside-down cake

2 tablespoons soft brown sugar
425 g (15 oz) tinned pear halves in syrup
250 g (9 oz/2 cups) self-raising flour
125 g (4½ oz) unsalted butter
185 g (6½ oz/¾ cup) caster (superfine) sugar
2 eggs, at room temperature, lightly beaten

Preheat the oven to 180°C (350°F/Gas 4). Lightly grease a 21 x 14 x 7 cm (8¼ x 5½ x 2¾ inch) loaf (bar) tin and line the base with baking paper. Sprinkle the brown sugar evenly over the base of the tin.

Drain the pears and reserve the syrup. Cut the pears in half and arrange, cut-side-down, over the base.

Sift the flour into a large bowl and make a well in the centre. Melt the butter and caster sugar in a small saucepan over low heat, stirring until the sugar has dissolved. Remove from the heat. Combine the egg with the reserved syrup. Add both the butter and the egg mixtures to the flour and stir with a wooden spoon until combined — do not overbeat. Spoon the mixture over the pears and smooth the surface.

Bake for 50 minutes, or until a skewer inserted into the centre of the cake comes out clean. Leave in the tin for 15 minutes, then turn out onto a wire rack to cool.

SERVES 6–8

Sand cake

185 g (6½ oz) unsalted butter, softened
2 teaspoons natural vanilla extract
230 g (8 oz/1 cup) caster (superfine) sugar
3 eggs, at room temperature
185 g (6½ oz/1½ cups) self-raising flour
60 g (2¼ oz/⅓ cup) rice flour
4 tablespoons milk

Icing
185 g (6½ oz/1½ cups) icing (confectioners') sugar
60 g (2¼ oz/¼ cup) passionfruit pulp
15 g (½ oz) unsalted butter

Preheat the oven to 180°C (350°F/Gas 4). Lightly grease a 23 cm (9 inch) square tin and line the base with baking paper.

Beat the butter, vanilla, sugar, eggs, flours and milk using electric beaters until combined. Continue to beat at medium speed for 3 minutes, or until thick and creamy.

Pour the mixture into the prepared tin and smooth the surface. Bake for 50 minutes, or until a skewer inserted into the centre of the cake comes out clean. Leave in the tin for 10 minutes, then turn out onto a wire rack to cool completely.

To make the passionfruit icing, combine the ingredients in a small bowl and stir together until smooth. Spread over the top of the cooled cake. Leave to set, then cut into squares.

SERVES 8–10

Passionfruit and lemon delicious slice

120 g (4 oz) unsalted butter,
  softened
60 g (2¼ oz/½ cup) icing
  (confectioners') sugar, sifted
½ teaspoon natural vanilla
  extract
185 g (6½ oz/1½ cups) plain
  (all-purpose) flour, sifted
1 teaspoon grated lemon zest
icing (confectioners') sugar,
  to dust

Filling
90 g (3¼ oz/¾ cup) plain
  (all-purpose) flour
½ teaspoon baking powder
65 g (2¼ oz/¾ cup) desiccated
  coconut
3 eggs, at room temperature
230 g (8 oz/1 cup) caster
  (superfine) sugar
170 g (6 oz) passionfruit pulp
2 tablespoons lemon juice
1 teaspoon grated lemon zest

Preheat the oven to 180°C (350°F/Gas 4). Lightly grease an 18 x 27 cm (7 x 10½ inch) rectangular shallow tin and line the base with baking paper, leaving the paper hanging over on the two long sides.

Cream the butter and icing sugar using electric beaters until pale and creamy, then add the vanilla. Fold in the flour and lemon zest with a large metal spoon. Press into the tin and bake for 15–20 minutes, or until lightly golden.

To make the filling, sift the flour and baking powder together and add the coconut. Lightly beat the eggs and sugar in a bowl, then add the passionfruit pulp, lemon juice and zest. Add the dry ingredients and stir until combined. Pour over the base and bake for 20 minutes, or until firm to the touch. Leave to cool in the tin. Dust with icing sugar and cut into pieces.

MAKES 18 PIECES

Coconut, ginger and lime cake

150 g (5½ oz) unsalted butter, softened
170 g (6 oz/¾ cup) caster (superfine) sugar
2 teaspoons grated lime zest
2 eggs, at room temperature, lightly beaten
55 g (2 oz/¼ cup) finely chopped glacé ginger
215 g (7½ oz/1¾ cups) self-raising flour
45 g (1½ oz/½ cup) desiccated coconut
185 ml (6 fl oz/¾ cup) milk
lime slices, to garnish (optional)
vanilla ice cream, to serve (optional)

Preheat the oven to 180°C (350°F/Gas 4). Lightly grease a 12 x 22 cm (4½ x 8½ inch) loaf (bar) tin and line the base with baking paper.

Beat the butter, sugar and lime zest in a bowl using electric beaters until pale and creamy. Add the egg gradually, beating well after each addition, then add the ginger. Fold in the sifted flour and the coconut alternately with the milk.

Spoon the mixture into the prepared tin and smooth the surface. Bake for about 50 minutes, or until a skewer inserted into the centre of the cake comes out clean. Leave in the tin for 5 minutes, then turn out onto a wire rack to cool completely. Garnish with lime slices and lime zest and serve with ice cream, if desired.

SERVES 8–10

Raisin butter cake

160 g (5¾ oz/1 cup) raisins
3 tablespoons rum
250 g (9 oz) soft brown sugar
250 g (9 oz) unsalted butter, softened
3 eggs, lightly beaten
310 g (11 oz/2½ cups) self-raising flour, sifted
185 ml (6 fl oz/¾ cup) buttermilk

Coffee buttercream
3 teaspoons instant coffee powder or granules
125 g (4½ oz) unsalted butter, softened
185 g (6½ oz/1½ cups) icing (confectioners') sugar, sifted
½ teaspoon natural vanilla extract
2 teaspoons milk

Preheat the oven to 180°C (350°F/Gas 4). Lightly grease a 23 cm (9 inch) round cake tin and line the base with baking paper.

Combine the raisins, rum and 1 tablespoon of brown sugar in a saucepan. Bring to the boil, reduce the heat and simmer for 30 seconds. Set aside to cool. Beat the butter and remaining brown sugar using electric beaters until creamy. Add the egg gradually, beating well after each addition. Fold in the flour and buttermilk in two batches, then fold in the raisin and rum mixture. Spoon the mixture into the tin and bake for 1 hour 30 minutes, or until a skewer inserted into the centre of the cake comes out clean. Leave in the tin for 10 minutes, then turn out onto a wire rack to cool.

To make the buttercream, dissolve the coffee in 2 tablespoons boiling water. Beat the butter and icing sugar using electric beaters until creamy. Add the vanilla, coffee mixture and milk and beat for 2 minutes, or until smooth. Spread over the cake.

SERVES 10

Apple teacake

150 g (5½ oz) unsalted butter, chopped
230 g (8 oz/1 cup) caster (superfine) sugar
2 eggs, at room temperature, lightly beaten
1 teaspoon natural vanilla extract
185 g (6½ oz/1½ cups) self-raising flour, sifted
185 g (6½ oz/¾ cup) vanilla-flavoured yoghurt
1 apple (granny smith), peeled, cored and thinly sliced
1 teaspoon ground cinnamon

Preheat the oven to 180°C (350°F/Gas 4). Lightly grease a deep 20 cm (8 inch) round cake tin and line the base with baking paper.

Beat 130 g (4½ oz) of the butter and 185 g (6½ oz/¾ cup) of the sugar using electric beaters until light and creamy. Gradually add the egg, beating well after each addition until combined. Add the vanilla extract. Fold in the flour, then the yoghurt and stir until smooth.

Spoon the mixture into the prepared tin and smooth the surface. Arrange the apple slices over the mixture in a circular pattern starting in the centre. Sprinkle with the cinnamon and remaining sugar. Melt the remaining butter, then drizzle over the top.

Bake for 1 hour, or until a skewer inserted into the centre of the cake comes out clean. Leave in the tin for 30 minutes, then turn out onto a wire rack to cool. If desired, combine a little extra cinnamon and sugar and sprinkle over the apple.

SERVES 8

Sour cherry cake

125 g (4½ oz) unsalted butter, softened
170 g (6 oz/¾ cup) caster (superfine) sugar
2 eggs, at room temperature, lightly beaten
95 g (3¼ oz/1 cup) ground almonds
125 g (4½ oz/1 cup) self-raising flour
60 g (2¼ oz/½ cup) plain (all-purpose) flour
125 ml (4 fl oz/½ cup) milk
680 g (1 lb 8 oz) pitted morello cherries, well drained
icing (confectioners') sugar, to dust

Preheat the oven to 180°C (350°F/Gas 4). Lightly grease and flour a 23 cm (9 inch) fluted baba tin, shaking out the excess flour.

Beat the butter and sugar using electric beaters until pale but not creamy. Add the egg gradually, beating well after each addition.

Stir in the ground almonds, then fold in the sifted flours alternately with the milk. Gently fold in the cherries. Spoon the mixture into the prepared tin and smooth the surface.

Bake for 50 minutes, or until a skewer inserted into the centre of the cake comes out clean. Leave to cool in the tin for 10 minutes, then turn out onto a wire rack to cool completely. Dust with icing sugar before serving.

SERVES 8–10

NOTE: This cake is best eaten on the day it is made.

Saffron spice cake

250 ml (9 fl oz/1 cup) freshly squeezed orange juice
1 tablespoon finely grated orange zest
¼ teaspoon saffron threads
3 eggs, at room temperature
155 g (5½ oz/1¼ cups) icing (confectioners') sugar
250 g (9 oz/2 cups) self-raising flour
370 g (13 oz/3⅔ cups) ground almonds
125 g (4½ oz) unsalted butter, melted
icing (confectioners') sugar, extra, to dust
thick (double/heavy) cream, to serve

Preheat the oven to 180°C (350°F/Gas 4). Lightly grease a 22 cm (8¾ inch) round cake tin and line the base with baking paper.

Combine the orange juice, zest and saffron in a small saucepan and bring to the boil. Lower the heat and simmer for 1 minute. Leave to cool.

Beat the eggs and icing sugar using electric beaters until light and creamy. Fold in the sifted flour, almonds, orange juice mixture and butter with a metal spoon until just combined and the mixture is just smooth. Spoon the mixture into the prepared tin.

Bake for 1 hour, or until a skewer inserted into the centre of the cake comes out clean. Leave in the tin for 15 minutes, then turn out onto a wire rack to cool completely. Dust with a little icing sugar and serve with cream.

SERVES 8

Fig and raspberry cake

185 g (6½ oz) unsalted butter
185 g (6½ oz/¾ cup) caster (superfine) sugar
1 egg, at room temperature
1 egg yolk, at room temperature
335 g (11¾ oz/2⅔ cups) plain (all-purpose) flour
1 teaspoon baking powder
4 figs, quartered
grated zest of 1 orange
200 g (7 oz/1⅔ cups) raspberries
2 tablespoons sugar

Preheat the oven to 180°C (350°F/Gas 4). Lightly grease a 23 cm (9 inch) spring-form cake tin.

Cream the butter and sugar in a bowl using electric beaters until light and pale. Add the egg and beat again. Sift the flour over the bowl and fold in with the baking powder and a pinch of salt. Chill for 15 minutes until firm enough to roll out.

Divide the dough in two and roll out one piece large enough to fit the base of the tin. Cover with the figs, orange zest and raspberries. Roll out the remaining dough and fit it over the filling. Lightly brush the dough with water and sprinkle with sugar.

Bake for 30 minutes, or until a skewer inserted into the centre of the cake comes out clean.

SERVES 6

NOTE: If fresh figs are not available, you can use the same amount of dried figs but you need to rehydrate them first. Simmer them in orange juice for 5 minutes until they are plumped up and soft.

Snickerdoodle slice

250 g (9 oz/2 cups) plain (all-purpose) flour
230 g (8 oz/1 cup) caster (superfine) sugar
1 tablespoon ground cinnamon
2 teaspoons baking powder
2 eggs, at room temperature
250 ml (9 oz/1 cup) milk
125 g (4½ oz) unsalted butter, melted
3 tablespoons sugar
3 teaspoons ground cinnamon, extra

Preheat the oven to 180°C (350°F/Gas 4). Lightly grease a 20 x 30 cm (8 x 12 inch) rectangular tin and line the base with baking paper, leaving the paper hanging over on the two long sides.

Sift together the flour, caster sugar, cinnamon and baking powder and make a well in the centre.

In a small bowl, whisk together the eggs and milk. Pour into the flour and mix with a metal spoon to roughly combine. Fold in the butter until smooth — do not overmix. Spoon half the mixture into the tin and smooth the surface.

Combine the sugar and extra cinnamon, and sprinkle two-thirds over the mixture in the tin. Gently spoon the remaining cake mixture over the top, then sprinkle the remaining cinnamon sugar over the surface. Bake for 25–30 minutes, or until firm. Cool in the tin for 20 minutes, then lift out onto a wire rack to cool completely.

MAKES 20 PIECES

Strawberry roulade

2 eggs, at room temperature
1 egg white, at room temperature
115 g (4 oz/½ cup) caster (superfine) sugar
90 g (3¼ oz/¾ cup) self-raising flour
1 tablespoon caster (superfine) sugar, extra
250 g (9 oz/1 cup) smooth ricotta cheese
1 teaspoon natural vanilla extract
40 g (1½ oz/⅓ cup) icing (confectioners') sugar
250 g (9 oz/1⅔ cups) strawberries, chopped

Preheat the oven to 200°C (400°F/Gas 6). Lightly grease a 26 x 30 cm (10 x 12 inch) shallow Swiss roll tin (jelly roll tin) and line the base with baking paper, leaving the paper hanging over on the two long sides.

Using electric beaters, beat the eggs, egg white and sugar in a large bowl on high speed for 5 minutes, or until light and foamy. Sift the flour into the bowl and fold in quickly and lightly.

Pour the mixture into the prepared tin and smooth the surface. Bake for 8–10 minutes, or until the sponge springs back when lightly touched. Lay a sheet of baking paper on a tea towel (dish towel) and sprinkle lightly with the extra caster sugar.

Turn the sponge out onto the sugared paper, remove the lining paper and, starting from a short end, roll up the sponge with the paper, using the tea towel as a guide. Cool for 30 minutes.

Mix the ricotta, vanilla and icing sugar together with a wooden spoon. Unroll the sponge and spread with the ricotta mixture, leaving a 2 cm (¾ inch) border at the far end. Scatter over the strawberries, then carefully re-roll the sponge. Trim the ends, and cut into slices to serve.

SERVES 8

Madeira cake

180 g (6½ oz) unsalted butter, softened
170 g (6 oz/¾ cup) caster (superfine) sugar
3 eggs, at room temperature, beaten
165 g (5¾ oz/1⅓ cups) self-raising flour, sifted
2 teaspoons finely grated lemon zest, plus extra, to garnish
1 teaspoon lemon juice
2 teaspoons caster (superfine) sugar, extra, to sprinkle
icing (confectioners') sugar, to dust

Preheat the oven to 160°C (315°F/Gas 2–3). Lightly grease and flour a deep 18 cm (7 inch) round cake tin.

Beat the butter and sugar using electric beaters until pale and creamy. Add the eggs gradually, beating well after each addition. Fold in the flour, lemon zest and juice until combined. Spoon into the prepared tin and smooth the surface. Sprinkle the extra caster sugar over the top.

Bake for 1 hour, or until a skewer inserted into the centre of the cake comes out clean. Allow to cool for 15 minutes in the tin, then turn out onto a wire rack to cool completely. Dust with icing sugar and garnish with lemon zest.

SERVES 6

STORAGE: This cake will keep for 4 days wrapped in foil.

Rum and raisin cake

155 g (5½ oz/1¼ cups) raisins
3 tablespoons dark rum
185 g (6½ oz/1½ cups) self-raising flour
150 g (5½ oz) unsalted butter, chopped
140 g (5 oz/¾ cup) soft brown sugar
3 eggs, at room temperature, lightly beaten
ice cream, to serve (optional)

Preheat the oven to 180°C (350°F/Gas 4). Lightly grease a deep 20 cm (8 inch) round cake tin and line the base with baking paper.

Soak the raisins in the rum in a small bowl for 10 minutes. Sift the flour into a large bowl and make a well in the centre.

Melt the butter and sugar in a small saucepan over low heat, stirring until the sugar has dissolved. Remove from the heat. Combine with the rum and raisin mixture and add to the flour with the egg. Stir with a wooden spoon until combined — do not overbeat. Spoon the mixture into the prepared tin and smooth the surface.

Bake for 40 minutes, or until a skewer inserted into the centre of the cake comes out clean. Turn out onto a wire rack to cool completely. Serve with ice cream, if desired.

SERVES 8

Pineapple pecan cake

80 g (2¾ oz) unsalted butter, softened
250 g (9 oz/1 cup) sugar
2 eggs, at room temperature, lightly beaten
185 g (6½ oz/1½ cups) plain (all-purpose) flour
1¾ teaspoons baking powder
40 g (1½ oz/⅓ cup) finely chopped pecan nuts, toasted
180 g (6½ oz/¾ cup) finely chopped glacé pineapple
170 ml (5½ fl oz/⅔ cup) milk
icing (confectioners') sugar, to dust

Preheat the oven to 180°C (350°F/Gas 4). Grease a 23 cm (9 inch) round cake tin and line the base with baking paper.

Beat the butter and sugar using electric beaters until combined. Add the egg and beat until pale and creamy.

Sift together the flour, baking powder and ¼ teaspoon salt. Add to the butter mixture with the pecans, pineapple and milk, then beat on low speed for 1 minute, or until almost smooth.

Spoon the mixture evenly into the prepared tin and smooth the surface. Bake for 1 hour, or until a skewer inserted into the centre of the cake comes out clean. Leave in the tin for 10 minutes, then turn out onto a wire rack to cool completely. Dust with icing sugar just before serving.

SERVES 8–10

NOTE: Glacé pineapple is available from health food stores.

Lemon semolina cake

6 eggs, at room temperature, separated
310 g (11 oz/1¼ cups) caster (superfine) sugar
2 teaspoons finely grated lemon zest
4 tablespoons lemon juice
90 g (3¼ oz/¾ cup) semolina
95 g (3¼ oz/1 cup) ground almonds
2 tablespoons self-raising flour
thick (double/heavy) cream, to serve

Preheat the oven to 170°C (325°F/ Gas 3). Lightly grease a 24 cm (9½ inch) spring-form cake tin and line the base with baking paper.

Beat the egg yolks, 250 g (9 oz/1 cup) of the sugar, the lemon zest and 2 tablespoons of the lemon juice in a large bowl using electric beaters for 8 minutes, or until thick and pale.

Beat the egg whites in a dry bowl using electric beaters until firm peaks form. Gently fold the whites into the egg yolk mixture alternately with the combined semolina, ground almonds and flour — do not overmix. Carefully pour into the prepared tin and smooth the surface.

Bake for 35–40 minutes, or until a skewer inserted into the centre of the cake comes out clean. Leave for 5 minutes in the tin, then turn out onto a wire rack to cool completely. Pierce a few holes in the cake with a skewer.

Place the remaining lemon juice and sugar in a small saucepan with 125 ml (4 fl oz/ ½ cup) of water. Stir over low heat until the sugar has dissolved. Increase the heat and simmer for 3 minutes, or until thick and syrupy. Pour the hot syrup over the cooled cake. Serve with thick cream.

SERVES 8–10

rich

Baked cheesecake

375 g (13 oz) plain sweet biscuits (cookies)
175 g (6 oz) unsalted butter, melted

Filling
500 g (1 lb 2 oz) cream cheese
200 g (7 oz) caster (superfine) sugar
4 eggs, at room temperature
300 ml (10½ fl oz) pouring (whipping) cream

2 tablespoons plain (all-purpose) flour
1 teaspoon ground cinnamon
¼ teaspoon grated nutmeg
1 tablespoon lemon juice
2 teaspoons vanilla extract

whipped cream, to serve
strawberries, to decorate
grated nutmeg, to sprinkle
ground cinnamon, to sprinkle

Preheat the oven to 180°C (350°F/Gas 4). Lightly grease a 23 cm (9 inch) shallow spring-form cake tin.

Process the biscuits in a food processor until they are crushed into fine crumbs. Add the melted butter and process for a further 10 seconds. Press the mixture into the base and side of the tin, then refrigerate for 1 hour.

Beat the cream cheese and sugar in a bowl using electric beaters, then add the eggs and cream and beat for about 4 minutes. Fold in the flour, cinnamon, nutmeg, lemon juice and vanilla. Pour the mixture into the chilled crust.

Bake in the oven for 1 hour, or until the cheesecake is golden brown on top. Turn off the heat and let the cake stand in the oven for 2 hours. Then open the oven door and let the cake stand for a further 1 hour. Refrigerate overnight. Serve topped with cream and strawberries and sprinkle with nutmeg and cinnamon.

SERVES 10

Chocolate banana cake

3 ripe bananas, mashed
170 g (6 oz/¾ cup) caster (superfine) sugar
185 g (6½ oz/1½ cups) self-raising flour
2 eggs, at room temperature, lightly beaten
3 tablespoons light olive oil
3 tablespoons milk
100 g (3½ oz) dark chocolate, grated
90 g (3¼ oz/¾ cup) walnuts, chopped
thick (double/heavy) cream, to serve (optional)

Preheat the oven to 180°C (350°F/Gas 4). Lightly grease a 10 x 20 cm (4 x 8 inch) loaf (bar) tin and line the base with baking paper.

Mix the mashed banana and sugar in a large bowl until just combined. Add the sifted flour, eggs, oil and milk. Stir gently for 30 seconds with a wooden spoon. Fold in the chocolate and walnuts.

Pour the mixture into the tin and bake for 55 minutes, or until a skewer inserted into the centre of the cake comes out clean. Leave in the tin for 5 minutes, then turn out onto a wire rack. Serve warm with cream, if desired.

SERVES 6–8

Double chocolate brownies

80 g (2¾ oz/2¾ oz) butter
40 g (1½ oz/⅓ cup) unsweetened cocoa powder
145 g (5 oz/⅔ cup) caster (superfine) sugar
2 eggs, at room temperature
60 g (2¼ oz/½ cup) plain (all-purpose) flour
½ teaspoon baking powder
100 g (3½ oz/½ cup) chocolate chips

Preheat the oven to 180°C (350°F/Gas 4). Lightly grease an 18 x 28 cm (7 x 11 inch) rectangular shallow tin and line the base with baking paper, leaving the paper hanging over on the two long sides.

Melt the butter in a saucepan over low heat. Remove from the heat and stir in the cocoa and sugar, then the eggs.

Put a sieve over the saucepan and tip in the flour and baking powder, along with a pinch of salt. Sift into the saucepan, then stir to combine. Stir in the chocolate chips.

Pour the mixture into the prepared tin and bake for 30 minutes, or until a skewer inserted into the centre comes out clean. Leave to cool in the tin, then lift out and cut into pieces.

MAKES 12

Passionfruit and coconut cheese slice

100 g (3½ oz) slivered almonds
125 g (4½ oz/1 cup) plain
  (all-purpose) flour
1 teaspoon baking powder
100 g (3½ oz) unsalted butter
115 g (4 oz/½ cup) caster
  (superfine) sugar, plus
    185 g (6½ oz/¾ cup) extra
2 eggs, plus 1 egg yolk
25 g (1 oz) desiccated coconut
750 g (1 lb 10 oz) cream cheese
185 ml (6 fl oz) coconut milk

3 teaspoons vanilla extract
½ teaspoon lemon juice
65 g (2¼ oz/¾ cup) flaked
  almonds, toasted

Topping
90 g (3¼ oz/¾ cup) icing
  (confectioners') sugar
40 g (1½ oz) unsalted butter
1 tablespoon cornflour
  (cornstarch)
2 tablespoons passionfruit juice

Process the almonds in a food processor. Sift the flour and baking powder into a bowl. Rub the butter into the flour. Stir in the almonds and sugar. Add the egg yolk. Mix, then shape into a ball. Flatten, cover in plastic wrap and refrigerate.

Preheat the oven to 170°C (325°F/Gas 3). Lightly grease a 30 x 20 cm (12 x 8 inch) rectangular shallow tin and line the base with baking paper, leaving the paper hanging over on the two long sides. Roll the dough out and press into the tin. Sprinkle over the coconut and press in. Bake for 10 minutes. Combine the cream cheese and the eggs in the food processor. Add coconut milk, vanilla, lemon juice and the extra sugar, and process. Pour over the base. Bake for 40 minutes. Cool in the tin.

To make the topping, mix the icing sugar and butter until smooth. Stir in the cornflour, then the passionfruit juice. Mix until smooth, then spread over the slice. Scatter over the toasted almonds. Leave to set, then cut into squares.

MAKES 24 PIECES

Grandmother's
pavlova

4 egg whites, at room temperature
230 g (8 oz/1 cup) caster (superfine) sugar
2 teaspoons cornflour (cornstarch)
1 teaspoon white vinegar
500 ml (17 fl oz/2 cups) whipping (pouring) cream
strawberries, to decorate
3 passionfruit, to decorate

Preheat the oven to 160°C (315°F/Gas 2–3). Line a 28 x 32 cm (11 x 13 inch) baking tray with baking paper.

Beat the egg whites and a pinch of salt in a dry bowl using electric beaters until stiff peaks form. Add the sugar gradually, beating constantly after each addition, until the mixture is thick and glossy and all the sugar has dissolved.

Fold in the cornflour and vinegar using a metal spoon. Spoon the mixture into a mound on the prepared tray. Lightly flatten the top of the pavlova and smooth the sides. (This pavlova should have a cake shape and be about 2.5 cm (1 inch) high.)

Bake for 1 hour, or until pale cream and crisp. Remove from the oven while warm and carefully turn upside down onto a plate. Allow to cool.

Lightly whip the cream until soft peaks form and spread over the soft centre. Decorate with the halved strawberries and the pulp from the passionfruit. Cut into wedges to serve.

SERVES 6

Rich dark chocolate cake

185 g (6½ oz) unsalted butter, chopped
250 g (9 oz/1½ cups) dark chocolate chips
215 g (7½ oz/1¾ cups) self-raising flour
40 g (1½ oz/⅓ cup) unsweetened cocoa powder
375 g (13 oz/1½ cups) caster (superfine) sugar
3 eggs, at room temperature, lightly beaten

Chocolate topping
20 g (¾ oz) unsalted butter, chopped
125 g (4½ oz) dark chocolate, chopped

Preheat the oven to 160°C (315°F/Gas 2–3). Lightly grease a 22 cm (8¾ inch) spring-form cake tin and line the base with baking paper.

Gently melt the butter and chocolate chips in a heatproof bowl set over a saucepan of simmering water, making sure that the bowl does not touch the water. Stir occasionally until the chocolate has melted.

Sift the flour and cocoa into a large bowl. Combine the melted butter and chocolate mixture, sugar and egg, then add 250 ml (9 oz/1 cup) water and mix well. Add to the flour and cocoa and stir until well combined.

Pour the mixture into the prepared tin and bake for 1 hour 30 minutes, or until a skewer inserted into the centre of the cake comes out clean. Leave in the tin for 15 minutes, then turn out onto a wire rack to cool completely.

To make the chocolate topping, gently melt the butter and chocolate in a heatproof bowl set over a saucepan of simmering water, making sure that the bowl does not touch the water. Stir occasionally until the chocolate has melted. Spread the topping over the cooled cake in a swirl pattern.

SERVES 10–12

Vanilla slice

500 g (1 lb 2 oz) ready-made puff pastry

230 g (8 oz/1 cup) caster (superfine) sugar

90 g (3¼ oz/¾ cup) cornflour (cornstarch)

60 g (2¼ oz/½ cup) custard powder (instant vanilla pudding mix)

1 litre (35 fl oz/4 cups) pouring (whipping) cream

60 g (2¼ oz) unsalted butter

2 teaspoons vanilla extract

3 egg yolks, at room temperature

Icing

185 g (6½ oz/1½ cups) icing (confectioners') sugar

60 g (2¼ oz) passionfruit pulp

15 g (½ oz) unsalted butter

Preheat the oven to 210°C (415°F/Gas 6–7). Lightly grease two baking trays with oil. Line the base and sides of a shallow 23 cm (9 inch) square cake tin with foil, leaving the foil hanging over on two opposite sides.

Divide the pastry in half, roll each piece to a 25 cm (10 inch) square 3 mm (¼ inch) thick and put on a baking tray. Prick all over with a fork and bake for 8 minutes, or until golden. Trim each pastry sheet to a 23 cm (9 inch) square. Put one sheet top-side-down in the cake tin. Combine the sugar, cornflour and custard powder in a saucepan. Add the cream, stirring over medium heat for 2 minutes, or until it boils and thickens. Add the butter and vanilla and stir until smooth. Remove from the heat and whisk in the egg yolks. Spread the custard over the pastry in the tin, then cover with the other pastry sheet, top-side-down. Cool completely.

To make the icing, combine the icing sugar, passionfruit pulp and butter in a bowl, and stir until smooth. Lift the slice out of the tin. Ice the top and leave to set before cutting with a serrated knife.

MAKES 9 PIECES

Strawberry and mascarpone slice

175 g (6 oz) unsalted butter, softened
80 g (2¾ oz/⅓ cup) caster (superfine) sugar
1 egg yolk, at room temperature
250 g (9 oz/2 cups) plain (all-purpose) flour, sifted
300 g (10½ oz/1⅓ cups) mascarpone cheese
60 g (2¼ oz/½ cup) icing (confectioners') sugar, sifted
1 tablespoon lemon juice
300 g (10½ oz/2 cups) strawberries, cut into quarters
50 g (1¾ oz) dark chocolate, chopped

Preheat the oven to 180°C (350°F/Gas 4). Lightly grease a 20 x 30 cm (8 x 12 inch) rectangular shallow tin and line the base with baking paper, leaving the paper hanging over on the two long sides.

Beat the butter and sugar using electric beaters until light and fluffy. Add the egg yolk and beat well. Fold in the sifted flour until well combined. Press firmly into the prepared tin and prick all over with a fork. Bake for 25 minutes, or until light brown. Cool completely.

Beat the mascarpone, icing sugar and juice with a wooden spoon until smooth. Stir in the strawberries. Spoon over the base and refrigerate for 3 hours, or until firm.

Gently melt the chocolate in a heatproof bowl set over a saucepan of simmering water, making sure that the bowl does not touch the water. Stir occasionally until the chocolate has melted. Drizzle over the slice, then cut into pieces.

MAKES 24 PIECES

Chocolate and almond torte

150 g (5½ oz) flaked or whole almonds, toasted
1 small brioche
300 g (10½ oz) dark chocolate
2 tablespoons brandy
150 g (5½ oz) unsalted butter
150 g (5½ oz) caster (superfine) sugar

4 eggs, at room temperature
1 teaspoon natural vanilla extract (optional)
200 g (7 oz) mascarpone cheese
unsweetened cocoa powder, to dust
crème fraîche, to serve

Preheat the oven to 170°C (325°F/Gas 4). Lightly grease a 23 cm (9 inch) spring-form cake tin.

Put the almonds and brioche in a food processor and process until the mixture resembles breadcrumbs. Tip some of the mixture into the tin and shake it around so that it forms a coating on the bottom and side of the tin.

Gently melt the chocolate and brandy in a heatproof bowl set over a saucepan of simmering water, making sure that the bowl does not touch the water. Stir occasionally until the chocolate has melted. Cool slightly.

Cream the butter and sugar in the food processor for a few minutes until light and pale. Add the melted chocolate, eggs, vanilla and mascarpone. Add the remaining nut mixture and mix well. Pour into the tin.

Bake for 50–60 minutes, or until just set. Leave in the tin for 15 minutes, then turn out onto a wire rack to cool Dust with a little cocoa and serve with crème fraîche.

SERVES 8

Hazelnut cream squares

4 eggs, at room temperature, separated
115 g (4 oz/½ cup) caster (superfine) sugar
60 g (2¼ oz/½ cup) self-raising flour
75 g (2½ oz/⅔ cup) ground hazelnuts
150 g (5½ oz) unsalted butter, softened
170 g (6 oz/½ cup) chocolate hazelnut spread
60 g (2¼ oz/½ cup) icing (confectioners') sugar, sifted
unsweetened cocoa powder, to dust

Preheat the oven to 180°C (350°F/Gas 4). Lightly grease a 20 cm (8 inch) shallow square cake tin and line the base with baking paper.

Beat the egg whites in a bowl using electric beaters until soft peaks form. Gradually add the sugar, beating until thick and glossy. Beat the egg yolks into the mixture, one at a time.

Sift the flour over the mixture, add the ground hazelnuts and fold in with a metal spoon. Melt 20 g (¾ oz) of the butter with 2 tablespoons boiling water in a small bowl, then fold into the sponge mixture. Pour the mixture into the prepared tin and bake for 25 minutes, or until cooked. Leave in the tin for 5 minutes, then turn out onto a wire rack to cool completely. Cut the sponge in half horizontally through the centre.

Beat the hazelnut spread and the remaining butter using electric beaters until creamy. Beat in the icing sugar, then gradually add 3 teaspoons of boiling water and beat until smooth. Fill the cake with the icing mixture and refrigerate until the filling is firm. Dust with the cocoa powder, then cut into squares.

MAKES 16

Individual white chocolate chip cakes

125 g (4½ oz) unsalted butter
185 g (6½ oz/¾ cup) caster
    (superfine) sugar
2 eggs, at room temperature,
    lightly beaten
1 teaspoon natural vanilla extract
250 g (9 oz/2 cups) self-raising
    flour, sifted
125 ml (4 fl oz/½ cup) buttermilk
280 g (10 oz/1⅔ cups) white
    chocolate chips
white chocolate, shaved,
    to decorate

**White chocolate cream
    cheese icing**
100 g (3½ oz) white chocolate
3 tablespoons pouring
    (whipping) cream
200 g (7 oz/¾ cup) cream
    cheese, softened
40 g (1½ oz/⅓ cup) icing
    (confectioners') sugar

Preheat the oven to 170°C (325°F/Gas 3). Lightly grease a 12-hole standard muffin tin.

Beat the butter and sugar in a bowl using electric beaters until creamy. Gradually add the egg, beating well after each addition. Add the vanilla and beat until combined. Fold in the flour alternately with the buttermilk, then fold in the chocolate chips. Fill each muffin hole three-quarters full with the mixture. Bake for 20 minutes, or until a skewer inserted into the centre of the cake comes out clean. Leave in the tins for 5 minutes, then turn out onto a wire rack to cool completely.

To make the icing, melt the chocolate and cream in a saucepan over low heat until smooth. Cool slightly, then add to the cream cheese and icing sugar and beat until smooth. Spread the icing over the cakes and top with white chocolate shavings.

MAKES 12

Rum and raisin slice

60 g (2¼ oz/½ cup) raisins
4 tablespoons dark rum
200 g (7 oz) dark chocolate, chopped
60 g (2¼ oz) unsalted butter, chopped
125 g (4½ oz/½ cup) caster (superfine) sugar
250 ml (9 fl oz/1 cup) thick (double/heavy) cream
125 g (4½ oz/1 cup) plain (all-purpose) flour
3 eggs, at room temperature, lightly beaten
unsweetened cocoa powder, to dust

Preheat the oven to 180°C (350°F/Gas 4). Lightly grease an 18 x 28 cm (7 x 11 inch) rectangular shallow tin and line the base with baking paper, leaving the paper hanging over on the two long sides.

Combine the raisins and rum. Gently melt the chocolate and butter in a heatproof bowl set over a saucepan of simmering water, making sure that the bowl does not touch the water. Stir occasionally until the chocolate has melted. Stir in the sugar and cream.

Sift the flour into a bowl. Add the raisins, chocolate mixture and eggs and mix well. Pour into the tin and smooth the surface. Bake for 25–30 minutes, or until just set. Cool completely, then refrigerate overnight. Cut into small pieces and sprinkle with cocoa powder to serve.

MAKES 20 PIECES

Devil's food cake

165 g (5¾ oz/1⅓ cups) plain (all-purpose) flour
85 g (3 oz/⅔ cup) unsweetened cocoa powder
1 teaspoon bicarbonate of soda (baking soda)
250 g (9 oz/1 cup) sugar
250 ml (9 fl oz/1 cup) buttermilk
2 eggs, at room temperature, lightly beaten
125 g (4½ oz) unsalted butter, softened
125 ml (4 fl oz/½ cup) pouring (whipping) cream
icing (confectioners') sugar, to dust
fresh berries, to garnish

Preheat the oven to 180°C (350°F/Gas 4). Lightly grease a deep 20 cm (8 inch) round cake tin and line the base with baking paper.

Sift the flour, cocoa and bicarbonate of soda into a large bowl. Add the sugar to the sifted dry ingredients. Combine the buttermilk, eggs and butter, then pour onto the dry ingredients. Beat using electric beaters on low speed for 3 minutes, or until just combined. Increase the speed to high and beat for 3 minutes, or until the mixture is free of lumps and increased in volume. Spoon the mixture into the prepared tin and smooth the surface.

Bake for 40–50 minutes, or until a skewer inserted into the centre of the cake comes out clean. Leave in the tin for 15 minutes, then turn out onto a wire rack to cool completely. Cut the cake in half horizontally and fill with whipped cream. Dust with icing sugar and garnish with fresh berries.

SERVES 8

STORAGE: Unfilled, the cake will keep for 3 days in an airtight container or up to 3 months in the freezer. The filled cake is best assembled and eaten on the day of baking.

Chocolate truffle macaroon slice

3 egg whites, at room temperature
170 g (6 oz/¾ cup) caster (superfine) sugar
180 g (6½ oz/2 cups) desiccated coconut
250 g (9 oz) dark chocolate, chopped
300 ml (10½ fl oz/1¼ cups) pouring (whipping) cream
1 tablespoon unsweetened cocoa powder

Preheat the oven to 180°C (350°F/Gas 4). Lightly grease a 20 x 30 cm (8 x 12 inch) rectangular shallow tin and line the base with baking paper, leaving the paper hanging over on the two long sides.

Beat the egg whites in a dry bowl using electric beaters until soft peaks form. Slowly add the sugar, beating well after each addition until stiff and glossy. Fold in the coconut. Spread into the tin and bake for 20 minutes, or until light brown. While still warm, press down lightly but firmly with a palette knife. Cool completely.

Gently melt the chocolate in a heatproof bowl set over a saucepan of simmering water, making sure that the bowl does not touch the water. Stir occasionally until the chocolate has melted. Cool slightly.

Beat the cream using electric beaters until thick. Gently fold in the chocolate until well combined — do not overmix. Spread evenly over the base and refrigerate for 3 hours, or until set. Lift from the tin and dust with cocoa before serving.

MAKES 24 PIECES

Coffee cupcakes

200 g (7 oz) unsalted butter, softened
125 g (4½ oz/⅔ cup) soft brown sugar
2 eggs, at room temperature
1 tablespoon coffee and chicory extract
155 g (5½ oz/1¼ cups) self-raising flour
100 ml (3½ fl oz) buttermilk
125 g (4½ oz/1 cup) icing (confectioners') sugar

Preheat the oven to 150°C (300°F/Gas 2). Line two 50 ml (1¾ fl oz) 12-hole cupcake trays with paper patty cases.

Beat 185 g (6½ oz) of the butter and the brown sugar using electric beaters until light and creamy. Add the eggs one at a time, beating well after each addition. Mix in 3 teaspoons of the coffee and chicory extract.

Fold the flour and a pinch of salt alternately with the buttermilk into the creamed mixture until combined. Spoon evenly into the patty cases and bake for 25–30 minutes, or until just springy to the touch. Leave to cool in the tray.

To make the icing, combine the remaining butter, remaining extract, the icing sugar and 1½ tablespoons boiling water in a small bowl. Spread a little icing over each cupcake with a palette knife until evenly covered. If desired, decorate with chocolate-coated coffee beans.

MAKES 24

Chocolate mud cake

125 g (4½ oz/1 cup) plain
(all-purpose) flour
125 g (4½ oz/1 cup) self-raising
flour
60 g (2¼ oz/½ cup) dark
unsweetened cocoa powder
½ teaspoon bicarbonate of soda
(baking soda)
625 g (1 lb 6 oz/2¾ cups) sugar

450 g (1 lb) dark chocolate,
chopped
450 g (1 lb) unsalted butter
125 ml (4 fl oz/½ cup)
buttermilk
2 tablespoons oil
2 tablespoons instant espresso
coffee granules or powder
4 eggs, at room temperature

Preheat the oven to 160°C (315°F/Gas 2–3). Lightly grease a deep 23 cm (9 inch) square cake tin. Line the base and sides with baking paper, extending at least 2 cm (¾ inches) above the rim.

Sift the flours, cocoa and bicarbonate of soda into a large bowl. Stir in the sugar and make a well in the centre. Put 250 g (9 oz) of the chocolate and 250 g (9 oz) of the butter in a saucepan. Add 185 ml (6 fl oz/¾ cup) of water and stir over low heat until melted. Stir the chocolate mixture into the dry ingredients using a large metal spoon.

Whisk together the buttermilk, oil, coffee and eggs and add to the mixture, stirring until smooth. Pour into the tin and bake for 1 hour 40 minutes, or until a skewer inserted into the centre of the cake comes out clean. Cool in the tin.

Combine the remaining chocolate and butter in a small saucepan and stir over low heat until smooth. Cool to room temperature, stirring often, until thick enough to spread. Spread the icing over the cake. Allow the icing to set slightly before serving.

SERVES 12

Lemon ricotta slice

220 g (7¾ oz/1¾ cups) plain (all-purpose) flour
1 teaspoon baking powder
180 g (6 oz) unsalted butter, melted
230 g (8 oz/1 cup) caster (superfine) sugar
4 eggs, at room temperature
350 g (12 oz/1⅓ cups) ricotta cheese
200 ml (7 fl oz/¾ cup) pouring (whipping) cream
2 tablespoons lemon zest
185 ml (6 fl oz/¾ cup) lemon juice
icing (confectioners') sugar, to dust

Preheat the oven to 180°C (350°F/Gas 4). Lightly grease a 20 x 30 cm (8 x 12 inch) rectangular shallow tin and line the base with baking paper, leaving the paper hanging over on the two long sides.

Put the flour, baking powder, butter and half of the caster sugar in a food processor and process in short bursts until the mixture comes together in a ball. Add 1 egg and process until combined.

Press the mixture into the tin. Bake for 15 minutes, then remove from the oven. Reduce the oven to 150°C (300°F/Gas 2).

Place the ricotta, cream, lemon zest and juice, the remaining sugar and remaining eggs in the food processor and process for 2 seconds. Pour onto the pastry base and bake for 25–30 minutes — the slice will still have a slight wobble at this stage. Cool slightly, then refrigerate for 2 hours to firm. Cut into pieces. Dust with icing sugar before serving.

MAKES 15 PIECES

Date chocolate torte

100 g (3½ oz/¾ cup) slivered almonds
120 g (4 oz) dark chocolate, coarsely chopped
120 g (4 oz/⅔ cup) dried dates, pitted
3 egg whites, at room temperature
125 g (4½ oz/½ cup) caster (superfine) sugar
125 ml (4 fl oz/½ cup) pouring (whipping) cream
2 teaspoons caster (superfine) sugar, extra
30 g (1 oz) dark chocolate, grated, extra

Preheat the oven to 180°C (350°F/Gas 4). Lightly grease a 22 cm (8½ inch) spring-form cake tin and line with foil.

Put the almonds and chocolate in a food processor and process until fine. Finely chop the dates with a sharp knife.

Beat the egg whites using electric beaters until soft peaks form. Slowly add the sugar and continue beating until dissolved. Fold in the almond and chocolate mixture, then the dates. Spoon the mixture into the tin and smooth the surface. Bake for 30–35 minutes, or until the mixture is set and starts to come away from the side. Cool in the tin, then turn out onto a serving plate.

Whip the cream and extra sugar until soft peaks form. Spread the cream over the top with a spatula. Sprinkle with the grated chocolate to decorate.

SERVES 6

STORAGE: This torte keeps well, without cream, for 5–6 days wrapped in foil. With cream, this is best eaten on the day of baking.

Flourless chocolate cake

500 g (1 lb 2 oz) dark chocolate, chopped
6 eggs, at room temperature
2 tablespoons Frangelico or brandy
165 g (5¾ oz/1½ cups) ground hazelnuts
250 ml (9 fl oz/1 cup) pouring (whipping) cream
icing (confectioners') sugar, to dust
thick (double/heavy) cream, to serve

Preheat the oven to 150°C (300°F/Gas 2). Lightly grease a deep 20 cm (8 inch) round cake tin and line the base with baking paper.

Gently melt the chocolate in a heatproof bowl set over a saucepan of simmering water, making sure that the bowl does not touch the water. Stir occasionally until the chocolate has melted.

Put the eggs in a large heatproof bowl and add the Frangelico. Set the bowl over a saucepan of simmering water, making sure that the bowl does not touch the water. Beat the mixture using electric beaters on high speed for 7 minutes, or until light and foamy. Remove from the heat.

Using a metal spoon, quickly and lightly fold the chocolate and ground nuts into the egg mixture until just combined. Fold in the whipped cream and pour into the cake tin. Put the cake tin in a shallow roasting tin. Pour hot water into the roasting tin to come halfway up the side of the cake tin. Bake for 1 hour, or until just set. Remove the cake tin from the oven and cool to room temperature.

Cover with plastic wrap and refrigerate overnight. Turn the cake out onto a plate and cut into slices. Dust with icing sugar and serve with cream.

SERVES 10

Baked lemon cheesecake

100 g (3½ oz) plain sweet biscuits (cookies), crushed
75 g (2½ oz) butter, melted
300 g (10½ oz) low-fat ricotta cheese
200 g (7 oz) light cream cheese
125 g (4½ oz/½ cup) caster (superfine) sugar
4 tablespoons lemon juice
2 tablespoons grated lemon zest
1 egg, at room temperature
1 egg white, at room temperature

Preheat the oven to 160°C (315°F/ Gas 2–3). Lightly grease an 18 cm (7 inch) spring-form cake tin and line the base with baking paper.

Combine the crushed biscuits and butter in a bowl. Press the mixture into the base of the tin, then refrigerate for 30 minutes.

Beat the ricotta, cream cheese, sugar, lemon juice and 3 teaspoons of lemon zest using electric beaters until smooth. Beat in the egg and egg white.

Pour the mixture into the tin and sprinkle the surface with the remaining lemon zest. Bake for 45 minutes — the centre will still be a little wobbly. Leave to cool, then chill for 5 hours before serving.

SERVES 8

Chocolate, almond and mixed peel cake

1 tablespoon mixed peel, chopped
150 g (5½ oz) dark chocolate pieces
95 g (3¼ oz/1 cup) ground almonds
60 g (2¼ oz/½ cup) self-raising flour
4 eggs, at room temperature, separated
115 g (4 oz/½ cup) caster (superfine) sugar
2 tablespoons warm milk
170 ml (5½ fl oz/⅔ cup) pouring (whipping) cream
icing (confectioners') sugar, to dust (optional)

Preheat the oven to 180°C (350°F/Gas 4). Lightly grease a 20 cm (8 inch) spring-form cake tin and line the base with baking paper.

Put the mixed peel and 100 g (3½ oz) of the chocolate in a food processor and process until finely ground. Add the almonds and flour and process to combine. Beat the egg yolks and sugar using electric beaters for 5 minutes, or until thick. Stir in the chocolate and peel mixture, then the milk.

Beat the egg whites in a bowl until soft peaks form. Fold the whites into the cake mixture. Pour the mixture into the tin and smooth the surface. Bake for 45 minutes, or until a skewer inserted into the centre of the cake comes out clean. Leave in the tin for 5 minutes, then turn out onto a wire rack to cool.

To make the filling, melt the chocolate in a heatproof bowl set over a saucepan of simmering water, making sure that the bowl does not touch the water. Cut the cake in half horizontally. Spread the bottom layer with the chocolate, then the whipped cream. Cover with the remaining layer of cake and, if desired, dust with icing sugar.

SERVES 6

Tiramisu cake

510 g (1 lb 2 oz) packet French vanilla cake mix
3 eggs, at room temperature
4 tablespoons vegetable oil
300 ml (10½ fl oz) pouring (whipping) cream
30 g (1 oz/¼ cup) icing (confectioners') sugar
250 g (9 oz) mascarpone cheese, chilled
100 ml (3½ fl oz) Kahlua
1½ tablespoons instant coffee granules or powder
grated chocolate, to decorate (optional)

Preheat the oven to 180°C (350°F/Gas 4). Lightly grease a 22 cm (8½ inch) square cake tin and line the base with baking paper.

Beat the cake mix, eggs, oil and 290 ml (10 fl oz) of water in a large bowl using electric beaters for 2 minutes, or until well combined.

Pour into the tin and bake for 35–40 minutes, or until a skewer inserted into the centre of the cake comes out clean. Leave in the tin for 5 minutes, then turn out onto a wire rack to cool completely.

Beat the cream and sugar with a whisk until stiff. Fold in the mascarpone and 2 teaspoons of the Kahlua. Combine the coffee and the remaining Kahlua, stirring until the coffee has dissolved.

Cut the cake in half horizontally. Place the base of the cake on a serving plate and brush liberally with the coffee mixture, then spread one third of the cream mixture on top. Top with the other layer of cake and brush with the remaining coffee mixture. Spread the remaining cream mixture over the top and sides. Sprinkle the surface with grated chocolate to serve.

SERVES 6–8

crumbly

Plum crumble cake

165 g (5¾ oz/¾ cup) raw (demerara) sugar
250 g (9 oz/2 cups) self-raising flour
150 g (5½ oz) unsalted butter
1 egg, at room temperature
825 g (1 lb 13 oz) tinned plums in syrup,
    drained and thinly sliced
1½ teaspoons ground cinnamon
100 g (3½ oz/⅔ cup) blanched almonds, chopped

Preheat the oven to 180°C (350°F/Gas 4). Lightly grease a 20 cm (8 inch) shallow sandwich tin and line the base with baking paper.

Blend the sugar, flour and butter in a food processor in short bursts until the mixture is combined and crumbly. Add the egg and process until well combined. Press half the mixture into the base of the tin. Arrange the plum slices evenly over the dough, then sprinkle with the cinnamon.

Knead the almonds lightly into the remaining dough, then press onto the plum layer. Bake for 50 minutes, or until a skewer inserted into the centre of the cake comes out clean. Leave in the tin for 15 minutes, then turn out onto a wire rack to cool slightly.

SERVES 8

Baby coffee and walnut sour cream cakes

75 g (2½ oz/¾ cup) walnuts
155 g (5½ oz/⅔ cup) soft brown sugar
125 g (4½ oz) unsalted butter, softened
2 eggs, at room temperature, lightly beaten
125 g (4½ oz/1 cup) self-raising flour
80 g (2¾ oz/⅓ cup) sour cream
1 tablespoon coffee and chicory extract

Preheat the oven to 160°C (315°F/Gas 2–3). Lightly grease two 12-hole 60 ml (2 fl oz/¼ cup) mini muffin tins.

Process the walnuts and 45 g (1½ oz/¼ cup) of the sugar in a food processor until the walnuts are roughly chopped into small pieces. Transfer to a bowl.

Cream the butter and remaining sugar together in the food processor until pale and creamy. With the motor running, gradually add the egg and process until smooth. Add the flour and blend until well mixed. Add the sour cream and extract and process until thoroughly mixed.

Spoon ½ teaspoon of the walnut and sugar mixture into the base of each muffin hole, followed by a teaspoon of the cake mixture. Sprinkle a little more walnut mixture over the top, a little more cake mixture and top with the remaining walnut mixture. Bake for 20 minutes, or until risen and springy to the touch. Leave in the tins for 5 minutes. Transfer to a wire rack to cool completely.

MAKES 24

Apricot and macaroon slice

100 g (3½ oz) unsalted butter
80 g (2¾ oz/⅓ cup) caster
  (superfine) sugar
1 egg, at room temperature
185 g (6½ oz/1½ cups) plain
  (all-purpose) flour
½ teaspoon baking powder

Filling
250 g (9 oz/1⅓ cups) dried
  apricots, roughly chopped
1 tablespoon Grand Marnier
2 tablespoons caster (superfine)
  sugar

Topping
100 g (3½ oz) unsalted butter
80 g (2¾ oz/⅓ cup) caster
  (superfine) sugar
1 teaspoon natural vanilla
  extract
2 eggs, at room temperature
270 g (9½ oz/3 cups) desiccated
  coconut
40 g (1½ oz/⅓ cup) plain
  (all-purpose) flour
½ teaspoon baking powder

Preheat the oven to 180°C (350°F/Gas 4). Lightly grease a 20 x 30 cm (8 x 12 inch) rectangular shallow tin and line with baking paper. Cream the butter and sugar using electric beaters until light and fluffy. Add the egg and beat well. Sift the flour and baking powder and fold into the butter mixture. Press into the tin and bake for 25 minutes, or until golden.

To make the filling, combine the apricots, Grand Marnier, sugar and 125 ml (4 fl oz/ ½ cup) boiling water in a bowl. Set aside for 30 minutes, then purée in a food processor. Spread evenly over the cooled base.

To make the topping, cream the butter, sugar and vanilla using electric beaters until light. Add the eggs, beating well after each addition. Fold in the coconut, flour and baking powder. Spoon onto the apricot. Bake for 20–25 minutes, or until golden.

MAKES 16 PIECES

Chocolate
hazelnut friands

200 g (7 oz/1½ cups) hazelnuts
185 g (6½ oz) unsalted butter
6 egg whites, at room temperature
155 g (5½ oz/1¼ cups) plain (all-purpose) flour
30 g (1 oz/¼ cup) unsweetened cocoa powder
250 g (9 oz/2 cups) icing (confectioners') sugar
icing (confectioners') sugar, extra, to dust

Preheat the oven to 200°C (400°F/Gas 6). Lightly grease twelve 125 ml (4 fl oz/ ½ cup) friand tins.

Spread the hazelnuts out on a baking tray and bake for 8–10 minutes, or until fragrant (take care not to burn them). Put in a tea towel (dish towel) and rub vigorously to loosen the skins. Discard the skins. Cool, then process in a food processor until finely ground.

Heat the butter in a small saucepan over medium heat for 3–4 minutes, or until it turns a deep golden colour. Strain any dark solids and set aside to cool.

Lightly whisk the egg whites in a bowl until frothy but not firm. Sift the flour, cocoa and icing sugar into a large bowl and stir in the ground hazelnuts. Make a well in the centre, add the egg whites and butter and mix until combined.

Spoon the mixture into the friand holes until three-quarters filled. Bake for about 25 minutes, or until a skewer inserted into the centre comes out clean. Leave in the tin for 2–3 minutes, then turn out onto a wire rack to cool completely. Dust with icing sugar to serve.

MAKES 12

Date caramel shortcake

125 g (4½ oz) unsalted butter, plus 10 g (¼ oz) extra
115 g (4 oz/½ cup) caster (superfine) sugar
1 teaspoon natural vanilla extract
1 egg, at room temperature
250 g (9 oz/2 cups) plain (all-purpose) flour
1 teaspoon baking powder
175 g (6 oz/1 cup) seedless dates, roughly chopped
1 tablespoon soft brown sugar
2 teaspoons unsweetened cocoa powder
icing (confectioners') sugar, to sprinkle

Preheat the oven to 180°C (350°F/Gas 4). Lightly grease an 18 x 27 cm (7 x 10¾ inch) rectangular shallow tin and line the base with baking paper, leaving the paper hanging over on the two long sides.

Beat the butter, sugar and vanilla using electric beaters until light and fluffy. Beat in the egg, then transfer to a bowl. Fold in the combined sifted flour and baking powder in batches with a metal spoon. Press half the dough into the tin. Form the other half into a ball, cover and refrigerate for 30 minutes.

Put the dates, brown sugar, cocoa, extra butter and 250 ml (9 fl oz/1 cup) of water in a saucepan and bring to the boil, stirring. Reduce the heat and simmer, stirring, for 12–15 minutes, or until the dates are soft and the water has been absorbed. Spread onto a plate and refrigerate to cool quickly.

Spread the filling over the pastry base with a metal spatula, then grate the remaining dough over the top. Bake for 35 minutes, or until light brown and crisp. Leave in the tin for 15 minutes, then lift out onto a wire rack. Sprinkle with icing sugar and cut into squares.

MAKES 12 PIECES

Butter almond torte

120 g (4 oz) unsalted butter, chopped
90 ml (3 fl oz) milk
2 eggs, at room temperature
1 teaspoon natural vanilla extract
250 g (9 oz/2 cups) caster (superfine) sugar
135 g (4¾ oz/1 cup) plain (all-purpose) flour
2 teaspoons baking powder
100 g (3½ oz/¾ cup) slivered almonds

Preheat the oven to 180°C (350°F/Gas 4). Line the base of a 22 cm (8¾ inch) spring-form cake tin with foil and lightly grease the base and side.

Heat 60 g (2¼ oz) of the butter and 4 tablespoons of the milk in a small saucepan until the butter has melted.

Beat the eggs, vanilla and 185 g (6½ oz/¾ cup) of the sugar using electric beaters until thick and creamy. Stir in the butter and milk mixture. Sift in 125 g (4½ oz) of the flour and the baking powder and stir to combine. Pour into the tin and bake for 50 minutes.

Melt the remaining butter in a small saucepan. Stir in the almonds with the remaining sugar, flour and milk and stir until combined. Quickly spoon the topping onto the cake (the centre will still be uncooked) starting from the outside edges and avoid piling the topping in the centre. Return to the oven for a further 10–15 minutes, or until golden and cooked through. Leave in the tin to cool, then turn out onto a wire rack.

SERVES 8–10

NOTE: This torte is great served as a dessert with whipped cream.

Panforte

110 g (3¾ oz/¾ cup) hazelnuts
110 g (3¾ oz/¾ cup) almonds
125 g (4½ oz/⅔ cup) candied
   mixed peel, chopped
100 g (3½ oz/⅔ cup) candied
   pineapple, chopped
grated zest of 1 lemon
75 g (2½ oz/⅔ cup) plain
   (all-purpose) flour
1 teaspoon ground cinnamon

¼ teaspoon ground coriander
¼ teaspoon ground cloves
¼ teaspoon grated nutmeg
pinch of white pepper
150 g (5½ oz/⅔ cup) sugar
4 tablespoons honey
50 g (1¾ oz) unsalted butter
icing (confectioners') sugar,
   to dust

Line a 20 cm (8 inch) spring-form cake tin with rice paper or baking paper and grease well.

Toast the nuts under a hot grill (broiler), turning so they brown on all sides, then leave to cool. Put the nuts in a bowl with the mixed peel, pineapple, lemon zest, flour and spices and toss together. Preheat the oven to 150°C (300°F/Gas 2).

Put the sugar, honey and butter in a saucepan and melt together. Cook the syrup until it reaches 118°C (245°F) on a sugar thermometer, or a little of it dropped into cold water forms a firm ball when moulded between your fingers.

Pour the syrup into the nut mixture and mix well, working fast. Pour into the prepared tin and smooth the surface. Bake for 35 minutes.

Cool in the tin until the cake firms up enough to remove the side of the tin. Peel off the paper and leave to cool completely. Dust the top with icing sugar.

SERVES 10

Apple shortcake

250 g (9 oz/2 cups) plain
(all-purpose) flour
1 teaspoon baking powder
125 g (4½ oz) unsalted butter,
chilled and chopped
55 g (2 oz/¼ cup) caster
(superfine) sugar, plus
2 tablespoons extra

1 egg, lightly beaten
1 tablespoon cold milk
4 small red apples, peeled,
quartered and cored
1 teaspoon ground cinnamon
1 tablespoon milk, extra
raw (demerara) sugar,
to sprinkle

Preheat the oven to 180°C (350°F/Gas 4). Lightly grease a baking tray and line with baking paper, leaving the paper hanging over on the two long sides.

Sift the flour and baking powder into a large bowl. Add the butter and rub with your fingers until the mixture resembles fine breadcrumbs. Stir in the sugar.

Make a well in the centre and add the combined egg and milk. Mix with a flat-bladed knife using a cutting action until the mixture comes together in beads. Gently gather together and lift out onto a lightly floured work surface. Press together into a ball, flatten slightly, cover in plastic wrap and chill for 20–30 minutes.

Halve the dough — keep one half in the refrigerator and roll the other half into an even 20 cm (8 inch) square. Put on the baking tray. Cut the apple quarters into thin slices and arrange in rows, to form a double layer of apples over the pastry. Sprinkle with the cinnamon and extra caster sugar.

Roll the remaining pastry into a 20 cm (8 inch) square and put over the apple. Brush with milk and sprinkle with sugar. Bake for 40–45 minutes, or until crisp and golden.

MAKES 9 PIECES

Rhubarb yoghurt cake

150 g (5½ oz/1¼ cups) finely sliced fresh rhubarb
310 g (11 oz/2½ cups) self-raising flour, sifted
250 g (9 oz/1 cup) caster (superfine) sugar
1 teaspoon natural vanilla extract
2 eggs, at room temperature, lightly beaten
125 g (4½ oz/½ cup) plain yoghurt
1 tablespoon rosewater
125 g (4½ oz) unsalted butter, melted

Preheat the oven to 180°C (350°F/Gas 4). Lightly grease a 23 cm (9 inch) round cake tin and line the base with baking paper.

Combine the rhubarb, flour and sugar in a bowl. Add the vanilla, egg, yoghurt, rosewater and melted butter, stirring until the mixture is just combined.

Spoon the mixture into the cake tin and bake for 1 hour, or until a skewer inserted into the centre of the cake comes out clean. Leave in the tin for 15 minutes, then turn out onto a wire rack to cool completely. Serve with yoghurt or cream.

SERVES 8

Cider crumble slice

60 g (2¼ oz) unsalted butter
1½ tablespoons golden or maple syrup
150 ml (5 fl oz/⅔ cup) alcoholic apple cider
250 g (9 oz/2 cups) self-raising flour
⅛ teaspoon ground ginger
50 g (1¾ oz/¼ cup) soft brown sugar
70 g (2½ oz/⅓ cup) pitted dates, chopped
150 g (5½ oz/1½ cups) walnuts, chopped
1 egg, at room temperature
1 large granny smith apple
2½ tablespoons caster (superfine) sugar
60 g (2¼ oz/½ cup) plain (all-purpose) flour

Preheat the oven to 170°C (325°F/Gas 3). Lightly grease a 20 x 30 cm (8 x 12 inch) rectangular shallow tin and line the base with baking paper, leaving the paper hanging over on the two long sides.

Melt 20 g (¾ oz) of the butter and the golden syrup in a saucepan. Remove from the heat and stir in the cider. Sift the flour and ginger into a bowl. Stir in the brown sugar, dates and half the nuts. Beat in the golden syrup mixture and egg until the mixture is smooth. Spoon into the tin.

Peel, core and thinly slice the apple, then cut into 1.5 cm (½ inch) pieces. Melt the remaining butter in a small saucepan. Add the caster sugar, flour, apple and remaining nuts and stir well. Spread over the cake mixture. Bake for 30 minutes, or until golden and a skewer inserted into the centre comes out clean. Cool in the tin, remove and cut into squares.

MAKES 24 PIECES

Walnut brownies

85 g (3 oz/⅔ cup) self-raising flour
85 g (3 oz/⅔ cup) unsweetened cocoa powder
250 g (9 oz/1 cup) caster (superfine) sugar
330 g (11½ oz) unsalted butter, melted
4 eggs, at room temperature, lightly beaten
1 teaspoon natural vanilla extract
250 g (9 oz/1½ cups) dark chocolate chips
125 g (4½ oz/1 cup) walnut pieces
icing (confectioners') sugar, to dust

Preheat the oven to 180°C (350°F/Gas 4). Lightly grease a 20 x 30 cm (8 x 12 inch) rectangular shallow tin and line the base with baking paper, leaving the paper hanging over on the two long sides.

Sift together the flour and cocoa, then add the sugar. Make a well in the centre, then add the butter, eggs and vanilla and beat using electric beaters until smooth. Fold in the chocolate chips and walnuts.

Spoon into the tin and smooth the surface. Bake for 25 minutes, or until a skewer inserted into the centre comes out clean. Leave in the tin for 10 minutes, then turn out onto a wire rack to cool completely. Dust with icing sugar.

MAKES 24 PIECES

Zucchini and walnut cake

245 g (8½ oz/2½ cups) walnuts
500 g (1 lb 2 oz) zucchini (courgettes)
250 ml (9 fl oz/1 cup) canola oil
330 g (11½ oz/1½ cups) raw (demerara) sugar
3 eggs, at room temperature
310 g (11 oz/2½ cups) self-raising flour, sifted
1½ teaspoons ground cinnamon
1 teaspoon ground nutmeg

Preheat the oven to 170°C (325°F/Gas 3). Lightly grease a 22 x 12 cm (8¾ x 4¾ inch) loaf (bar) tin and line the base with baking paper, leaving the paper hanging over on the two long sides.

Roughly chop 185 g (6½ oz/1¾ cups) of the walnuts. Grate the zucchini, then put the zucchini in a large bowl with the oil, sugar, eggs and chopped walnuts and mix well. Stir in the flour, cinnamon and nutmeg.

Spoon the mixture into the tin and arrange the remaining walnuts on top. Bake for 1 hour 10 minutes, or until a skewer inserted into the centre of the cake comes out clean. Leave in the tin for 15 minutes, then turn out onto a wire rack to cool completely. Cut into slices and serve.

SERVES 6–8

STORAGE: Wrap in foil when cooled. The cake will keep for 4–5 days.

Hawaiian
macadamia cake

375 g (13 oz/3 cups) self-raising
flour
1 teaspoon ground cinnamon
375 g (13 oz/1½ cups) caster
(superfine) sugar
90 g (3¼ oz/1 cup) desiccated
coconut
5 eggs, lightly beaten
440 g (15½ oz) tinned crushed
pineapple in syrup
375 ml (13 fl oz/1½ cups)
vegetable oil

100 g (3½ oz/⅔ cup)
macadamia nuts, chopped

Lemon cream cheese icing
60 g (2¼ oz/¼ cup) cream
cheese, softened
30 g (1 oz) unsalted butter,
softened
1 tablespoon lemon juice
185 g (6½ oz/1½ cups) icing
(confectioners') sugar, sifted

Preheat the oven to 180°C (350°F/Gas 4). Lightly grease a deep 23 cm (9 inch) round cake tin. Line the base and side with two sheets of baking paper, cutting it to sit 2–3 cm (¾–1 inch) above the side of the tin.

Sift the flour and cinnamon into a large bowl. Add the sugar and coconut and stir to combine. Add the eggs, pineapple and oil and mix well. Stir in the macadamias.

Spoon the mixture into the prepared tin and smooth the surface. Bake for 1 hour 15 minutes, or until a skewer inserted into the centre of the cake comes out clean. Leave in the tin for 30 minutes, then turn out onto a wire rack to cool completely.

To make the lemon cream cheese icing, beat the cream cheese and butter in a small bowl using electric beaters. Add the lemon juice and icing sugar and beat until smooth. Spread over the cooled cake.

SERVES 10–12

Pecan brownies

125 g (4½ oz) dark chocolate, chopped
90 g (3¼ oz) unsalted butter, softened
230 g (8 oz/1 cup) caster (superfine) sugar
1 teaspoon natural vanilla extract
2 eggs, at room temperature
80 g (2¾ oz/⅔ cup) plain (all-purpose) flour
30 g (1 oz/¼ cup) unsweetened cocoa powder
½ teaspoon baking powder
125 g (4½ oz) pecan nuts, roughly chopped

Preheat the oven to 180°C (350°F/Gas 4). Lightly grease a 17 cm (6¾ inch) square tin and line the base with baking paper, leaving the paper hanging over on the two long sides.

Gently melt the chocolate in a heatproof bowl set over a saucepan of simmering water, making sure that the bowl does not touch the water. Stir occasionally until the chocolate has melted. Cool slightly.

Beat the butter, sugar and vanilla using electric beaters until thick and creamy. Beat in the eggs one at a time, beating well after each addition. Stir in the chocolate.

Fold in the sifted combined flour, cocoa and baking powder with a metal spoon, then fold in the pecans. Spoon into the tin and smooth the surface. Bake for 30–35 minutes, or until firm and it comes away from the sides of the tin. Leave to cool in the tin, then lift out onto a wire rack. Cut into squares.

MAKES 16 PIECES

Blueberry shortcake

100 g (3½ oz/¾ cup) hazelnuts
280 g (10 oz/2¼ cups) self-raising flour
1½ teaspoons ground cinnamon
165 g (5¾ oz/¾ cup) raw (demerara) sugar
150 g (5½ oz) unsalted butter, chopped
2 eggs, at room temperature
160 g (5¾ oz/½ cup) blueberry jam
1 tablespoon demerara sugar, extra
fresh blueberries, to garnish (optional)

Preheat the oven to 180°C (350°F/Gas 4). Lightly grease a deep 20 cm (8 inch) round cake tin and line the base with baking paper.

Spread the hazelnuts on a baking tray and roast for 5–10 minutes, or until lightly golden. Put in a tea towel (dish towel) and rub together to remove the skins, then roughly chop.

Mix the flour, cinnamon, sugar, butter and half the hazelnuts in a food processor in short bursts until finely chopped. Add the eggs and process until well combined. Press half the mixture onto the base of the tin, then spread the jam evenly over the mixture. Lightly knead the remaining hazelnuts into the remaining dough, then press evenly over the jam layer.

Sprinkle the extra sugar over the top and bake for 50 minutes, or until a skewer inserted into the centre of the cake comes out clean. Leave in the tin for 15 minutes, then turn out onto a wire rack to cool completely. Garnish with fresh blueberries, if desired, and serve with cream.

SERVES 8–10

Walnut cake with chocolate icing

185 g (6½ oz) unsalted butter
95 g (3¼ oz/½ cup) soft brown sugar
2 eggs, at room temperature
185 g (6½ oz/1½ cups) self-raising flour
90 g (3¼ oz/¾ cup) walnuts, chopped
3 tablespoons milk

Chocolate icing
125 g (4½ oz) dark chocolate, chopped
20 g (¾ oz) unsalted butter

Preheat oven to 180°C (350°F/Gas 4). Lightly grease a 20 cm (8 inch) spring-form cake tin and line the base with baking paper.

Beat the butter and sugar in a large bowl using electric beaters for 5 minutes, or until thick and creamy. Add the eggs one at a time, beating well after each addition. Fold in the flour and 60 g (2¼ oz/½ cup) of the walnuts alternately with the milk until just combined. Spoon the mixture into the prepared tin and smooth the surface.

Bake for 35 minutes, or until a skewer inserted into the centre of the cake comes out clean. Leave in the tin for 5 minutes, then turn out onto a wire rack to cool.

To make the chocolate icing, gently melt the chocolate and butter iin a heatproof bowl set over a saucepan of simmering water, making sure that the bowl does not touch the water. Stir occasionally until the chocolate has melted. Cool slightly, then spread over the cake. Sprinkle with the remaining walnuts.

SERVES 6

Fruit and seed slice

200 g (7 oz) unsalted butter

175 g (6 oz/½ cup) golden or maple syrup

125 g (4½ oz/½ cup) crunchy peanut butter

2 teaspoons natural vanilla extract

30 g (1 oz/¼ cup) plain (all-purpose) flour

30 g (1 oz/⅓ cup) ground almonds

½ teaspoon mixed (pumpkin pie) spice

300 g (10½ oz/3 cups) quick-cooking oats

2 teaspoons finely grated orange zest

185 g (6½ oz/1 cup) soft brown sugar

45 g (1½ oz/½ cup) desiccated coconut

50 g (1¾ oz/⅓ cup) sesame seeds, toasted

90 g (3¼ oz/½ cup) pepitas (pumpkin seeds) or
shelled sunflower seeds

80 g (2¾ oz/½ cup) raisins, chopped

45 g (1½ oz/¼ cup) mixed peel

Preheat the oven to 170°C (325°F/Gas 3). Lightly grease a 20 x 30 cm (8 x 12 inch) rectangular shallow tin and line the base with baking paper, leaving the paper hanging over on the two long sides.

Heat the butter and golden syrup in a small saucepan over low heat, stirring occasionally until melted. Remove from the heat and stir in the peanut butter and vanilla until combined.

Mix together the remaining ingredients, stirring well. Make a well in the centre and add the butter and syrup mixture. Mix with a large metal spoon until combined. Press evenly into the tin and bake for 25 minutes, or until golden and firm. Leave to cool in the tin, then lift out and cut into squares.

MAKES 18 PIECES

White Christmas

45 g (1½ cups) puffed rice cereal
100 g (3½ oz/1 cup) milk powder
125 g (4½ oz/1 cup) icing (confectioners') sugar
90 g (3¼ oz/1 cup) desiccated coconut
80 g (2¾ oz/⅓ cup) chopped red glacé cherries
80 g (2¾ oz/⅓ cup) chopped green glacé cherries
55 g (1¾ oz/½ cup) sultanas (golden raisins)
250 g (9 oz) copha (white vegetable shortening)

Line a 18 x 28 cm (7 x 11 inch) rectangular shallow tin with foil.

Combine the puffed rice, milk powder, icing sugar, coconut, glacé cherries and sultanas in a large bowl. Make a well in the centre.

Melt the copha in a saucepan over low heat. Cool slightly, then add to the well in the puffed rice mixture. Stir with a wooden spoon.

Spoon the mixture into the prepared tin and smooth down the surface. Refrigerate for 30 minutes, or until completely set. Remove from the tin, and peel away and discard the foil. Cut into 24 small triangles to serve.

MAKES 24 PIECES

Choc-chip and pistachio friands

150 g (5½ oz) shelled pistachio nuts
60 g (2¼ oz/½ cup) plain (all-purpose) flour
175 g (6 oz) unsalted butter
210 g (7½ oz/1⅔ cups) icing (confectioners') sugar
2 tablespoons unsweetened cocoa powder
½ teaspoon ground cardamom
5 egg whites, at room temperature, lightly whisked
200 g (7 oz) chocolate chips
icing (confectioners') sugar, to dust

Preheat the oven to 200°C (400°F/Gas 6). Lightly grease and line ten 125 ml (4 fl oz/ ½ cup) friand tins.

Put the pistachios on a baking tray and roast for 5 minutes. Remove from the oven and allow to cool. Place the pistachios and flour in a food processor and process until finely ground.

Beat the butter and icing sugar in a bowl using electric beaters until light and creamy. Sift together the pistachios and flour with the cocoa and cardamom, and fold into the creamed mixture.

Stir the egg whites into the creamed mixture, together with the chocolate chips, and mix to combine. Spoon the mixture into the prepared tins and bake for 25–30 minutes, or until the friands come away from the sides of the tin. Cool on wire racks. Dust lightly with icing sugar.

MAKES 10

Poppy seed slice

135 g (4¾ oz/1 cup) plain
  (all-purpose) flour
75 g (2½ oz) unsalted butter,
  chopped, plus 125 g (4½ oz)
  extra
60 g (2¼ oz/¼ cup) caster
  (superfine) sugar
1 egg yolk, at room
  temperature
40 g (1½ oz/¼ cup) poppy seeds
2 tablespoons milk, warmed

90 g (3¼ oz/⅓ cup) caster
  (superfine) sugar, extra
1 teaspoon grated lemon zest
1 egg
90 g (3¼ oz/¾ cup) plain
  (all-purpose) flour, extra,
125 g (4½ oz/1 cup) icing
  (confectioners') sugar
½ teaspoon finely grated lemon
  zest, extra
1 tablespoon lemon juice

Preheat the oven to 180°C (350°F/Gas 4). Lightly grease an 11 x 35 cm (4¼ x 13¾ inch) loose-based flan tin.

Sift the flour into a bowl and rub in the butter until it resembles breadcrumbs. Stir in the sugar. Make a well in the centre and then add 2–3 teaspoons water and the egg yolk. Mix until it comes together in beads. Press into a ball and flatten slightly. Cover in plastic wrap and chill for 15 minutes. Roll out the dough to fit the base and sides of the tin. Trim the edges. Cover the base with baking paper and fill with baking beads or uncooked rice. Bake for 10 minutes. Remove the paper and beads and bake for 5 minutes. Soak the poppy seeds in the milk for 10 minutes.

Beat the extra butter and sugar together with the zest using electric beaters until fluffy. Beat in the egg and stir in the poppy seed mixture and extra flour. Spread over the pastry. Bake for 25 minutes, or until brown.

Combine the icing sugar, extra zest and enough juice to form a paste. Spread over the slice and cool.

MAKES 14 PIECES

Orange, pistachio and semolina slice

100 g (3½ oz/⅔ cup) shelled pistachio nuts
200 g (7 oz) unsalted butter, chopped
160 g (5¾ oz/⅔ cup) caster (superfine) sugar, plus
   250 g (9 oz/1 cup) extra
1 teaspoon natural vanilla extract
1 tablespoon finely grated orange zest
2 eggs, at room temperature
60 g (2¼ oz/½ cup) self-raising flour, sifted
125 ml (4 fl oz/½ cup) orange juice
185 g (6½ oz/1½ cups) fine semolina
125 ml (4 fl oz/½ cup) orange juice, extra
icing (confectioners') sugar, to dust

Preheat the oven to 180°C (350°F/Gas 4). Lightly grease a 20 x 30 cm (8 x 12 inch) rectangular shallow tin and line the base with baking paper, leaving the paper hanging over on the two long sides.

Roast the pistachios for 8–10 minutes, or until they are toasted. Cool, then chop. Beat the butter and sugar using electric beaters until light and fluffy. Add the vanilla, orange zest and eggs, and beat until combined. Add the flour, orange juice, semolina and pistachios, and fold in with a spatula until just combined. Spread into the tin. Bake for 30 minutes, or until golden brown. Leave in the tin for 10 minutes, then turn out onto a wire rack to cool.

Mix the extra sugar and orange juice in a small saucepan. Bring to the boil over medium heat, then simmer for 1 minute. Spoon over the slice. Cool and cut into squares or diamonds. Dust with icing sugar.

MAKES 18 PIECES

Peanut toffee shortbread

290 g (10¼ oz) unsalted butter
115 g (4 oz/½ cup) caster (superfine) sugar
1 egg, at room temperature
185 g (6½ oz/1½ cups) plain (all-purpose) flour, sifted
60 g (2¼ oz/½ cup) self-raising flour, sifted
180 g (6½ oz/1 cup) soft brown sugar
2 tablespoons golden or maple syrup
½ teaspoon lemon juice
400 g (14 oz/2½ cups) roasted unsalted peanuts

Preheat the oven to 180°C (350°F/Gas 4). Lightly grease an 18 x 27 cm (7 x 10½ inch) rectangular shallow tin and line the base with baking paper, leaving the paper hanging over on the two long sides.

Cream 110 g (3¾ oz) of butter and the caster sugar using electric beaters until light and fluffy. Add the egg and beat well. Fold in the sifted flours with a large metal spoon until just combined. Press into the tin and bake for 15 minutes, or until firm and lightly coloured. Cool for 10 minutes.

Place the brown sugar, golden syrup, lemon juice and remaining butter in a saucepan. Stir over low heat until the sugar has dissolved. Simmer, stirring, for 5 minutes. Stir in the peanuts. Spread evenly over the base using two spoons — be careful as the mixture is very hot. Bake for a further 5 minutes. Leave to cool in the tin for 15 minutes, then turn out and cut into fingers.

MAKES 18 PIECES

Honey, banana and macadamia cake

125 g (4½ oz) unsalted butter, chopped
440 g (15½ oz/1¼ cups) honey
310 g (11 oz/2½ cups) self-raising flour
1½ teaspoons mixed (pumpkin pie) spice
3 or 4 large carrots, coarsely grated
1 large ripe banana, mashed
120 g (4¼ oz/¾ cup) macadamia nuts, chopped
3 eggs, at room temperature, lightly beaten

Ricotta honey icing
375 g (13 oz/1½ cups) smooth ricotta cheese
70 g (2½ oz) unsalted butter, softened
2 tablespoons honey

Preheat the oven to 180°C (350°F/Gas 4). Lightly grease a 26 cm (10¼ inch) round cake tin and line the base with baking paper.

Melt the butter and honey in a saucepan, stirring until combined. Leave to cool. Sift the flour and mixed spice into a large bowl. Add the carrot, banana, macadamias, egg and honey mixture, stirring until the mixture is just combined and smooth.

Spoon the mixture into the prepared tin and bake for 1 hour 10 minutes, or until a skewer inserted into the centre of the cake comes out clean. Leave in the tin for 15 minutes, then turn out onto a wire rack to cool completely.

To make the ricotta honey icing, beat the ricotta, butter and honey using electric beaters for 2–3 minutes, or until light and creamy. Spread the icing over the top the cake.

SERVES 8–10

Sesame and ginger slice

125 g (4½ oz/1 cup) plain (all-purpose) flour
½ teaspoon bicarbonate of soda (baking soda)
1 teaspoon ground ginger
¼ teaspoon mixed (pumpkin pie) spice
2 eggs, at room temperature
140 g (5 oz/¾ cup) soft brown sugar
125 g (4½ oz) unsalted butter, melted
55 g (2 oz/¼ cup) chopped crystallized ginger
50 g (1¾ oz/⅓ cup) sesame seeds, toasted

Preheat the oven to 180°C (350°F/Gas 4). Lightly grease a 20 x 30 cm (8 x 12 inch) rectangular shallow tin and line the base with baking paper, leaving the paper hanging over on the two long sides.

Sift together the flour, bicarbonate of soda, ginger, mixed spice and ¼ teaspoon salt. Beat the eggs and brown sugar in a large bowl using electric beaters for 2 minutes, or until thick and creamy. Mix in the melted butter and gently fold in the flour mixture. Add the crystallized ginger and half the sesame seeds and mix gently.

Spread into the tin and sprinkle evenly with the remaining sesame seeds. Bake for 20 minutes, or until firm to touch and slightly coloured. Leave in the tin for 10 minutes, then lift out onto a wire rack to cool completely.

MAKES 15 PIECES

No-bake chocolate squares

100 g (3½ oz) shortbread biscuits, roughly crushed
120 g (4¼ oz) pistachio nuts, shelled
150 g (5½ oz) hazelnuts, toasted and skinned
100 g (3½ oz) glacé cherries, roughly chopped
300 g (10½ oz) dark chocolate, chopped
200 g (7 oz) unsalted butter, chopped
1 teaspoon instant coffee granules or powder
2 eggs, at room temperature, lightly beaten

Lightly grease an 18 x 27 cm (7 x 10¾ inch) rectangular shallow tin and line the base with baking paper, leaving the paper hanging over on the two long sides.

Combine the biscuits, pistachios, 90 g (3¼ oz) of the hazelnuts, and half of the cherries.

Gently melt the chocolate and butter in a heatproof bowl set over a saucepan of simmering water, making sure that the bowl does not touch the water. Stir occasionally until the chocolate has melted. Remove the bowl from the pan and when the mixture has cooled slightly, mix in the coffee and eggs. Pour over the nut mixture and mix well.

Pour the mixture into the tin and pat down well. Roughly chop the remaining hazelnuts and sprinkle over the top with the remaining cherries. Refrigerate overnight.

Remove from the tin and trim the edges of the slice before cutting into pieces. Keep in the refrigerator.

MAKES 18 PIECES

Coconut and pineapple slice

20 g (¾ oz) shredded coconut
90 g (3¼ oz/¾ cup) self-raising flour
50 g (1¾ oz/½ cup) plain (all-purpose) flour
140 g (5 oz/¾ cup) soft brown sugar
2 tablespoons sunflower seeds
2 tablespoons sesame seeds
70 g (2½ oz/½ cup) chopped macadamia nuts
60 g (2¼ oz) chopped dates
1 tablespoon chopped glacé ginger

45 g (1½ oz/½ cup) desiccated coconut
230 g (8 oz) tinned crushed pineapple, drained
100 g (3½ oz) unsalted butter
2 eggs, at room temperature, lightly beaten

Icing
250 g (9 oz/2 cups) icing (confectioners') sugar
30 g (1 oz) unsalted butter, melted
1½ tablespoons lemon juice

Preheat the oven to 170°C (325°F/Gas 3). Spread the shredded coconut on a baking tray and toast for 5–8 minutes, or until golden. Lightly grease a 20 x 30 cm (8 x 12 inch) rectangular shallow tin and line the base with baking paper, leaving the paper hanging over on the two long sides.

Sift the flours into a bowl. Add the brown sugar, seeds, macadamias, dates, ginger and desiccated coconut. Stir in the pineapple, melted butter and beaten egg, and mix well. Spoon the mixture into the tin. Bake for 25 minutes, or until golden. Cool.

To make the icing, combine the icing sugar, butter and lemon juice in a bowl. Stir in 1–2 teaspoons of boiling water. Spread evenly over the slice. Sprinkle the top with the toasted shredded coconut.

MAKES 24 PIECES

Polenta cake

45 g (1½ oz/⅓ cup) sultanas (golden raisins)
2 tablespoons brandy
225 g (8 oz/1 cup) ricotta cheese
250 g (9 oz/1 cup) caster (superfine) sugar
225 g (8 oz/1½ cups) polenta
pinch of grated nutmeg
½ teaspoon grated lemon zest
¼ teaspoon natural vanilla extract
20 g (¾ oz) unsalted butter, chilled and cut into small cubes
2 tablespoons pine nuts
icing (confectioners') sugar, to dust
whipped cream, to serve

Put the sultanas and brandy in a small bowl with enough water to cover them and leave for 30 minutes. Drain and dry well on paper towel.

Preheat the oven to 160°C (315°F/Gas 2–3). Lightly grease a 25 cm (10 inch) loose-bottomed or spring-form cake tin with a tight-fitting base.

Beat the ricotta and 450 ml (16 fl oz) of cold water in a large bowl using electric beaters until smooth. Add the sugar and beat until smooth, then stir in the polenta, nutmeg, lemon zest, vanilla and sultanas.

Pour the mixture into the tin. Dot the surface with butter and sprinkle the pine nuts on top. Put the tin on a baking tray to catch any drips and bake for about 1 hour 30 minutes, or until golden and set. Dust with icing sugar. Serve warm or cold with whipped cream.

SERVES 8–10

Honey picnic cake

300 g (10½ oz/1¼ cups) sour cream
165 g (5¾ oz/¾ cup) soft brown sugar
1 egg, at room temperature
300 g (10½ oz/2 cups) wholemeal plain (all-purpose) flour
1 teaspoon baking powder
3 tablespoons honey, warmed
50 g (1¾ oz/½ cup) pecan nuts, chopped

Preheat the oven to 150°C (300°F/Gas 2). Lightly grease a 22 x 12 cm (8¾ x 4¾ inch) loaf (bar) tin and line the base with baking paper, leaving the paper hanging over on the two long sides.

Blend the sour cream, sugar and egg in a food processor until combined. Add the flour and baking powder and process until well blended. Add the honey and process until mixed. Add the nuts and process just long enough for them to mix through.

Spoon into the prepared tin and bake for 1 hour, or until a skewer inserted into the centre of the cake comes out clean. Leave in the tin for 15 minutes, then turn out onto a wire rack to cool completely.

SERVES 8–10

NOTE: This cake is delicious served plain or buttered.

Pistachio, yoghurt and cardamom cake

150 g (5½ oz/1 cup) unsalted pistachio nuts
½ teaspoon ground cardamom
150 g (5½ oz) unsalted butter, chopped
185 g (6½ oz/1½ cups) self-raising flour
310 g (11 oz/1¼ cups) caster (superfine) sugar
3 eggs, at room temperature
125 g (4½ oz/½ cup) plain yoghurt
1 lime

Preheat the oven to 180°C (350°F/Gas 4). Lightly grease a 20 cm (8 inch) round cake tin and line the base with baking paper.

Place the pistachios and cardamom in a food processor and pulse until just chopped. Add the butter, flour and 185 g (6½ oz/¾ cup) of the caster sugar and pulse for 20 seconds, or until crumbly. Add the combined eggs and yoghurt and pulse for 10 seconds, or until just combined. Spoon into the tin and smooth the surface.

Bake for 45–50 minutes, or until a skewer inserted into the centre of the cake comes out clean.

To make the syrup, peel the zest off the lime with a vegetable peeler — remove any white pith from the zest. Place the remaining caster sugar and 100 ml (3½ fl oz) of water in a saucepan and stir over low heat until the sugar has dissolved. Bring to the boil, then add the lime zest and cook for 5 minutes. Strain and cool slightly. Pierce the cake with a few skewer holes and pour the hot syrup over the cooled cake.

SERVES 8

Chocolate peanut squares

200 g (7 oz) dark chocolate, chopped
125 g (4½ oz) unsalted butter
230 g (8 oz/1 cup) soft brown sugar
65 g (2¼ oz/¼ cup) crunchy peanut butter
2 eggs, at room temperature
125 g (4½ oz/1 cup) plain (all-purpose) flour
30 g (1 oz/¼ cup) self-raising flour
80 g (2¾ oz/½ cup) unsalted roasted peanuts, roughly chopped
100 g (3½ oz) dark chocolate, extra, broken into pieces

Preheat the oven to 170°C (325°F/Gas 3). Lightly grease an 18 x 27 cm (7 x 10½ inch) rectangular tin and line the base with baking paper, leaving the paper hanging over on the two long sides.

Gently melt the chocolate in a heatproof bowl set over a saucepan of simmering water, making sure that the bowl does not touch the water. Stir occasionally until the chocolate has melted. Allow to cool.

Cream the butter, sugar and peanut butter using electric beaters until thick. Add the eggs one at a time, beating well after each addition. Stir in the chocolate, sifted flours and peanuts.

Spread the mixture into the tin and gently press the pieces of dark chocolate evenly into the surface. Bake for 30 minutes, or until a skewer inserted into the centre comes out clean. Cool in the tin.

MAKES 24 PIECES

Toffee walnut slice

250 g (9 oz/1⅓ cups) pitted dates, roughly chopped
1 teaspoon bicarbonate of soda (baking soda)
215 g (7½ oz) unsalted butter
185 g (6½ oz/1½ cups) self-raising flour
1 teaspoon natural vanilla extract
1 teaspoon baking powder
3 eggs, at room temperature
90 ml (3 fl oz/⅓ cup) milk
2 tablespoons soft brown sugar
90 g (3¼ oz/¾ cup) icing (confectioners') sugar
90 g (3¼ oz/¾ cup) chopped walnuts

Preheat the oven to 180°C (350°F/Gas 4). Lightly grease a 20 x 30 cm (8 x 12 inch) rectangular tin and line the base with baking paper, leaving the paper hanging over on the two long sides.

Place the dates in a saucepan with 200 ml (7 fl oz) water, bring to the boil, then reduce the heat and simmer for 10 minutes. Add the bicarbonate of soda and cool.

Place 185 g (6½ oz) of the butter, the flour, vanilla, baking powder, eggs and 75 ml (2½ fl oz) of the milk in a food processor and mix in short bursts for 1 minute, or until well blended. Add the dates and pulse to blend. Do not overprocess.

Place the mixture in the tin and bake for 20 minutes, or until a skewer inserted in the centre comes out clean. Set aside to cool.

Place the remaining butter and milk and the brown sugar in a pan and heat to dissolve the sugar. Add the icing sugar and mix. Spread over the cooled slice and sprinkle with the walnuts.

MAKES 18 PIECES

sticky

Bakewell slice

125 g (4½ oz/1 cup) plain
 (all-purpose) flour
30 g (1 oz/¼ cup) icing
 (confectioners') sugar
170 g (6 oz) unsalted butter,
 chilled and chopped
1 egg yolk
115 g (4 oz/½ cup) caster
 (superfine) sugar

4 eggs, at room temperature
125 g (4½ oz/1¼ cups) ground
 almonds
2 drops almond extract
160 g (5¾ oz/½ cup) raspberry
 jam
25 g (1 oz/¼ cup) flaked
 almonds

Preheat the oven to 180°C (350°F/Gas 4). Lightly grease a 20 x 30 cm (8 x 12 inch) rectangular shallow tin and line the base with baking paper, leaving the paper hanging over on the two long sides.

Sift the flour and 1 tablespoon of the icing sugar into a bowl, add 50 g (1¾ oz) of the butter and rub it in until the mixture resembles breadcrumbs. Add the egg yolk and 2 tablespoons cold water and mix with a flat-bladed knife until the mixture comes together in beads. Gather into a ball, cover with plastic wrap and refrigerate for 30 minutes. Roll out between two sheets of baking paper, remove the paper and put in the tin, pressing into the edges. Bake for 10 minutes. Leave to cool.

Beat the remaining butter and the caster sugar using electric beaters until creamy. Add the eggs and fold in the ground almonds and almond extract. Spread the jam over the pastry base and pour over the filling. Sprinkle with almonds and bake for 30–35 minutes, or until firm. Leave to cool.

Sift the remaining icing sugar into a bowl and mix in 2–3 teaspoons of warm water to form a free-flowing paste. Drizzle over the slice in a zigzag pattern and leave to set. Trim the edges and cut into squares.

MAKES 15 PIECES

Caramel peach cake

250 g (9 oz) unsalted butter, softened
60 g (2¼ oz/⅓ cup) soft brown sugar
825 g (1 lb 13 oz) tinned peach halves in natural juice
250 g (9 oz/1 cup) caster (superfine) sugar
3 teaspoons finely grated lemon zest
3 eggs, at room temperature, lightly beaten
310 g (11 oz/2½ cups) self-raising flour, sifted
250 g (9 oz/1 cup) plain yoghurt

Preheat the oven to 180°C (350°F/Gas 4). Lightly grease a deep 23 cm (9 inch) round cake tin and line the base with baking paper.

Melt 50 g (1¾ oz) of the butter and pour on the base of the tin. Evenly sprinkle the brown sugar over the top. Drain the peaches, reserving 1 tablespoon of the liquid. Arrange the peach halves, cut-side-up, over the sugar mixture.

Beat the caster sugar, lemon zest and remaining butter using electric beaters for 5–6 minutes, or until pale and creamy. Add the egg gradually, beating well after each addition. Using a metal spoon, fold in the flour alternately with the yoghurt (in two batches), then the reserved peach liquid. Spoon the mixture over the peaches and smooth the surface.

Bake for 1 hour 25 minutes, or until a skewer inserted into the centre of the cake comes out clean. Leave in the tin for 30 minutes, then turn out onto a large serving plate.

SERVES 10–12

Individual sticky date cakes

270 g (9½ oz/1½ cups) pitted dates, chopped
1 teaspoon bicarbonate of soda (baking soda)
150 g (5½ oz) unsalted butter, chopped
185 g (6½ oz/1½ cups) self-raising flour
265 g (9½ oz) soft brown sugar
2 eggs, at room temperature, lightly beaten
2 tablespoons golden or maple syrup
185 ml (6 fl oz/¾ cup) pouring (whipping) cream

Preheat the oven to 180°C (350°F/Gas 4). Lightly grease six 250 ml (9 fl oz/1 cup) muffin holes.

Put the dates and 250 ml (9 fl oz/1 cup) of water in a saucepan, bring to the boil, then remove from the heat and stir in the bicarbonate of soda. Add 60 g (2¼ oz) of the butter and stir until melted. Sift the flour into a large bowl, add 125 g (4½ oz/⅔ cup) of the sugar and stir. Make a well in the centre, add the date mixture and egg and stir until just combined.

Spoon evenly into the muffin holes and bake for 20 minutes, or until a skewer inserted into the centre of the cake comes out clean.

To make the sauce, put the golden syrup, cream, the remaining butter and the remaining sugar in a small saucepan and stir over low heat for 3–4 minutes, or until the sugar has dissolved. Bring to the boil, then reduce the heat and simmer, stirring occasionally, for 2 minutes. To serve, turn the cakes onto serving plates, pierce the cakes a few times with a skewer and drizzle with the sauce. Serve with ice cream, if desired.

MAKES 6

Carrot, spice and sour cream cake

310 g (11 oz/2½ cups) self-
   raising flour
2 teaspoons ground cinnamon
1 teaspoon ground nutmeg
150 g (5½ oz/¾ cup) dark
   brown sugar
250 g (9 oz) carrots, grated
4 eggs, at room temperature
250 g (9 oz/1 cup) sour cream
250 ml (9 fl oz/1 cup) vegetable
   oil

**Orange cream cheese
frosting**
60 g (2¼ oz/¼ cup) cream
   cheese, softened
20 g (¾ oz) unsalted butter,
   softened
1 teaspoon grated orange zest
2 teaspoons orange juice
125 g (4½ oz/1 cup) icing
   (confectioners') sugar

Preheat the oven to 160°C (315°F/Gas 2–3). Lightly grease a deep 22 cm (8¾ inch) round tin and line the base with baking paper.

Sift the flour and spices into a large bowl, then stir in the brown sugar and grated carrot until well mixed.

Combine the eggs, sour cream and oil until lightly beaten. Add to the carrot mixture and stir until well combined. Spoon the mixture into the prepared tin and smooth the surface. Bake for 1 hour 15 minutes, or until a skewer inserted into the centre of the cake comes out clean. Leave in the tin for 10 minutes, then turn out onto a wire rack to cool completely.

To make the frosting, beat the cream cheese, butter, zest and juice in a bowl using electric beaters until light and fluffy. Gradually beat in the icing sugar until smooth. Spread over the cooled cake.

SERVES 8–10

Lemon squares

125 g (4½ oz) unsalted butter
75 g (2½ oz/⅓ cup) caster (superfine) sugar
155 g (5½ oz/1¼ cups) plain (all-purpose) flour, sifted
icing (confectioners') sugar, to dust

Topping
4 eggs, at room temperature, lightly beaten
250 g (9 oz/1 cup) caster (superfine) sugar
3 tablespoons lemon juice
1 teaspoon finely grated lemon zest
30 g (1 oz/¼ cup) plain (all-purpose) flour
½ teaspoon baking powder

Preheat the oven to 180°C (350°F/Gas 4). Lightly grease a 20 x 30 cm (8 x 12 inch) rectangular shallow tin and line the base with baking paper, leaving the paper hanging over on the two long sides.

Cream the butter and sugar using electric beaters until pale and fluffy. Fold in the flour with a metal spoon. Press into the tin and bake for 20 minutes, or until golden and firm. Leave to cool.

Beat the eggs and sugar using electric beaters for 2 minutes, or until light and fluffy. Stir in the lemon juice and lemon zest. Sift together the flour and baking powder and gradually whisk into the egg mixture. Pour onto the base. Bake for 25 minutes, or until just firm. Leave to cool in the tin. Cut into squares and dust with icing sugar before serving.

MAKES 30 PIECES

Pineapple
upside-down cake

20 g (¾ oz) unsalted butter, melted
2 tablespoons soft brown sugar
440 g (15½ oz) tinned pineapple rings in natural juice
90 g (3¼ oz) unsalted butter, extra, softened
115 g (4 oz/½ cup) caster (superfine) sugar
2 eggs, at room temperature, lightly beaten
1 teaspoon natural vanilla extract
125 g (4½ oz/1 cup) self-raising flour

Preheat the oven to 180°C (350°F/Gas 4). Lightly grease a 20 cm (8 inch) ring tin. Pour the melted butter into the base of the tin and tip to evenly coat. Sprinkle with the brown sugar.

Drain the pineapple and reserve 4 tablespoons of the juice. Cut the pineapple rings in half and arrange on the base.

Beat the extra butter and the caster sugar using electric beaters until light and creamy. Gradually add the egg, beating well after each addition. Add the vanilla and beat until combined. Fold in the flour alternately with the reserved juice, using a metal spoon.

Spoon the mixture evenly over the pineapple and smooth the surface. Bake for 35–40 minutes, or until a skewer inserted into the centre of the cake comes out clean. Leave in the tin for 10 minutes, then turn out onto a wire rack to cool completely.

SERVES 6–8

Orange and almond syrup cake

2 large navel oranges
6 eggs, separated
1 tablespoon orange blossom
  water or orange liqueur
230 g (8 oz/1 cup) caster
  (superfine) sugar
300 g (10½ oz/3 cups) ground
  almonds
1 teaspoon baking powder

3 navel oranges, peeled, pith
  removed, sliced, to garnish

Orange syrup
500 ml (17 fl oz/2 cups) fresh
  orange juice, strained
185 g (6½ oz/¾ cup) caster
  (superfine) sugar
3 tablespoons Sauternes

Grease and lightly flour a 23 cm (9 inch) spring-form cake tin, tipping out any excess flour. Put the whole oranges into a saucepan full of water. Boil for 2 hours, topping up with water as needed. Remove the oranges, quarter them and process in a food processor until smooth. Cool thoroughly. Preheat the oven to 180°C (350°F/Gas 4).

Place the egg yolks, orange blossom water and caster sugar in a large bowl and beat until smooth, then stir in the orange purée and mix well. Whisk the egg whites in a dry bowl until firm peaks form. Add the ground almonds and baking powder to the orange mixture, stir well, then fold in the egg whites. Pour into the cake tin and bake for 1 hour, or until firm. Cool in the tin, then transfer to a serving plate.

To make the syrup, put the orange juice, sugar and Sauternes in a saucepan over medium heat and stir until the sugar is dissolved. Reduce the heat and simmer for 20 minutes, or until reduced by half and slightly syrupy, skimming off any scum.

Cut the cake into wedges, garnish with orange slices and drizzle with the syrup. Serve with cream, if desired.

SERVES 6–8

Glacé fruit slice

480 g (1 lb 1 oz/2 cups) roughly chopped glacé fruit
2 tablespoons rum, plus 1 teaspoon extra
100 g (3½ oz) unsalted butter, softened
90 g (3¼ oz/⅓ cup) caster (superfine) sugar
2 eggs, at room temperature
2 teaspoons natural vanilla extract
125 g (4½ oz/1 cup) mixed toasted nuts, roughly chopped
30 g (1 oz/¼ cup) plain (all-purpose) flour, sifted
30 g (1 oz/¼ cup) self-raising flour, sifted
25 g (1 oz/¼ cup) milk powder
80 g (2¾ oz/⅔ cup) icing (confectioners') sugar

Preheat the oven to 190°C (375°F/Gas 5). Lightly grease an 18 x 27 cm (7 x 10½ inch) rectangular shallow tin and line the base with baking paper, leaving the paper hanging over on the two long sides.

Combine the glacé fruit and rum in a bowl. Beat the butter and sugar using electric beaters until light and fluffy. Add the eggs one at a time, beating well after each addition. Beat in the vanilla, then stir in the fruit mixture, nuts, flours and milk powder.

Spread evenly into the tin. Bake for 15 minutes, then reduce the oven to 180°C (350°F/Gas 4) and bake for 10 minutes, or until golden brown. Cool in the tin until just warm.

Combine the icing sugar, extra rum and 1 teaspoon water until smooth. Spread over the slice and cool completely. Cut into three lengthways strips, then cut each strip into eight pieces.

MAKES 24 PIECES

Chocolate caramel slice

200 g (7 oz) plain chocolate biscuits (cookies), crushed
100 g (3½ oz) unsalted butter, melted
2 tablespoons desiccated coconut
125 g (4½ oz) unsalted butter, extra
400 ml (14 fl oz) tinned sweetened condensed milk
90 g (3¼ oz/⅓ cup) caster (superfine) sugar
3 tablespoons maple syrup
250 g (9 oz) dark chocolate, chopped
2 teaspoons oil

Lightly grease a 20 x 30 cm (8 x 12 inch) rectangular shallow tin and line the base with baking paper, leaving the paper hanging over on the two long sides.

Combine the biscuits, melted butter and coconut in a bowl, then press into the tin and smooth the surface.

Combine the butter, condensed milk, sugar and maple syrup in a small saucepan. Stir over low heat for 15 minutes, or until the sugar has dissolved and the mixture is smooth, thick and lightly coloured. Remove from the heat and cool slightly. Pour over the biscuit base and smooth the surface. Refrigerate for 30 minutes, or until firm.

Gently melt the chocolate in a heatproof bowl set over a saucepan of simmering water, making sure that the bowl does not touch the water. Stir occasionally until the chocolate has melted. Add the oil and stir until smooth. Spread over the caramel and leave until partially set before marking into 24 triangles. Refrigerate until firm. Cut into triangles before serving.

MAKES 24 TRIANGLES

Golden syrup and ginger pear cake

175 g (6 oz/½ cup) golden or maple syrup
250 g (9 oz/2 cups) self-raising flour
2½ teaspoons ground ginger
165 g (5¾ oz/¾ cup) soft brown sugar
2 pears (about 200 g/7 oz), peeled, halved and thinly sliced
3 eggs, at room temperature, lightly beaten
125 ml (4 fl oz/½ cup) buttermilk
150 g (5½ oz) unsalted butter, chopped

Preheat the oven to 180°C (350°F/Gas 4). Lightly grease a deep 18 cm (7 inch) round cake tin and line the base with baking paper. Pour half of the golden syrup over the base of the tin, spreading evenly with a metal spoon, which has been run under hot water.

Sift the flour and ground ginger into a bowl. Add the sugar and pear, then the egg, buttermilk and 125 g (4½ oz) of the butter, melted, and stir until just combined and smooth.

Spoon the mixture into the prepared tin and bake for 1 hour 30 minutes, or until a skewer inserted into the centre of the cake comes out clean. Leave in the tin for 10 minutes, then carefully invert onto a serving plate.

Heat the remaining golden syrup and the remaining butter in a saucepan over low heat until the butter has melted. Spoon the sauce evenly over the cake and serve warm. Serve with ice cream or cream, if desired.

SERVES 8

Mini passionfruit
almond cakes with lime glaze

60 g (2¼ oz/⅓ cup) ground almonds
2 tablespoons plain (all-purpose) flour, sifted
100 g (3½ oz) icing (confectioners') sugar, plus extra to dust
1 teaspoon finely grated lime zest
pulp from 1 passionfruit
120 g (4¼ oz) unsalted butter, melted
2 eggs, at room temperature
2 tablespoons lime juice

Preheat the oven to 170°C (325°F/Gas 3). Lightly grease eight 30 ml (1 oz) patty tins. Place the ground almonds, flour, 60 g (2¼ oz) icing sugar, lime zest, passionfruit pulp and half the butter in a bowl. Separate the eggs, reserve 1 egg yolk and discard the other. Beat the egg whites in a clean, dry bowl using electric beaters to soft peaks. Gently fold into the almond mixture. Spoon into the prepared patty tins and bake for 10–15 minutes, or until the cakes are puffed and golden.

Meanwhile, place the lime juice, remaining butter and sifted remaining icing sugar in a small saucepan, and heat to a simmer, stirring until all the sugar has dissolved. Remove from the heat and cool slightly, then whisk in the reserved egg yolk. Return to very low heat and stir for 5 minutes, or until thickened. Do not boil.

Leave in the tin for 5 minutes, then gently remove. Serve two cakes per person, dusted with extra icing sugar and drizzled with a little lime curd. Serve with cream or ice cream, if desired.

SERVES 4

Orange and lemon syrup cake

3 lemons
3 oranges
250 g (9 oz) unsalted butter, chilled and chopped
685 g (1 lb 8 oz/3 cups) caster (superfine) sugar
6 eggs, at room temperature, lightly beaten
375 ml (13 fl oz/1½ cups) milk
375 g (13 oz/3 cups) self-raising flour, sifted

Preheat the oven to 160°C (315°F/Gas 2–3). Lightly grease a 24 cm (9½ inch) spring-form cake tin and line the base and side with baking paper.

Finely grate the zest from the lemons and oranges to give 3 tablespoons of each, then squeeze the fruit to give 185 ml (6 fl oz/¾ cup) juice from each. Heat the butter, 500 g (1 lb 2 oz/2 cups) of the sugar and 1 tablespoon each of the lemon and orange zest in a saucepan over low heat, stirring until melted. Pour into a bowl.

Add half the egg, 185 ml (6 fl oz/¾ cup) of the milk and 185 g (6½ oz/1½ cups) of the flour to the bowl, beating using electric beaters until just combined. Add the remaining egg, milk and flour and beat until smooth — do not overmix. Pour into the tin and bake for 1 hour 15 minutes, or until a skewer inserted into the centre of the cake comes out clean. Leave to cool in the tin.

Combine the fruit juices, the remaining zest and sugar and 125 ml (4 fl oz/½ cup) of water in a saucepan and stir over low heat until the sugar has dissolved. Increase the heat and bring to the boil for 10 minutes, or until the syrup thickens and reduces slightly. Pour the hot syrup over the cake. Cool in the tin for 10 minutes, then remove.

SERVES 10–12

Fig and cinnamon slice

125 g (4½ oz) unsalted butter, softened
55 g (2 oz/¼ cup) soft brown sugar
1 teaspoon ground cinnamon
185 g (6½ oz/1½ cups) plain (all-purpose) flour
375 g (13 oz/2⅓ cups) dried figs
1 cinnamon stick
125 g (4½ oz/½ cup) caster (superfine) sugar

Preheat the oven to 180°C (350°F/Gas 4). Lightly grease an 18 x 27 cm (7 x 10¾ inch) rectangular shallow tin and line the base with baking paper, leaving the paper hanging over on the two long sides.

Beat the butter, brown sugar and cinnamon using electric beaters until light and fluffy, then fold in the flour with a large metal spoon. Press the mixture evenly into the tin and bake for 25 minutes. Cool slightly.

Place the dried figs, cinnamon stick, caster sugar and 375 ml (13 fl oz/1½ cups) of boiling water in a saucepan, mix together and bring to the boil. Reduce the heat and simmer for 20 minutes, or until the figs have softened and the water has reduced by a third. Remove the cinnamon stick and place the mixture in a food processor. Process in short bursts until smooth.

Pour onto the cooked base and bake for 10 minutes, or until set. Leave to cool in the tin, then lift out and cut into squares.

MAKES 15 SQUARES

Gingerbread apricot upside-down cake

200 g (7 oz/¾ cup) glacé apricots
175 g (6 oz) unsalted butter
30 g (1 oz/⅓ cup) pecan nuts, finely chopped
165 g (5¾ oz/¾ cup) soft brown sugar
90 g (3¼ oz/¼ cup) golden or maple syrup
185 g (6½ oz/1½ cups) self-raising flour
3 teaspoons ground ginger
½ teaspoon ground nutmeg

Preheat the oven to 180°C (350°F/Gas 4). Lightly grease and flour the base of a deep 20 cm (8 inch) round cake tin, shaking out the excess flour.

Arrange the apricots around the base of the tin, cut-side-up. Melt the butter in a small saucepan over low heat. Transfer 1 tablespoon of the melted butter to a small bowl. Add the pecans and 55 g (2 oz/¼ cup) of the brown sugar and mix well. Sprinkle the mixture over the apricots.

Add the golden syrup and 125 ml (4 fl oz/½ cup) of water to the saucepan of melted butter and stir over medium heat until well combined. Sift the flour and spices in a bowl, then stir in the remaining sugar. Pour in the golden syrup mixture and mix well. Spoon the mixture over the apricots and smooth the surface.

Bake for 35–40 minutes, or until a skewer inserted into the centre of the cake comes out clean. Leave in the tin for 15 minutes, then turn out onto a wire rack to cool completely. Serve with custard, if desired.

SERVES 6

STORAGE: This cake keeps for 4 days in an airtight cake tin.

Chocolate and glacé cherry slice

125 g (4½ oz/1 cup) plain
(all-purpose) flour
40 g (1½ oz/⅓ cup)
unsweetened cocoa powder
90 g (3¼ oz/⅓ cup) caster
(superfine) sugar
125 g (4½ oz) unsalted butter
1 teaspoon vanilla extract
420 g (15 oz/2 cups) glacé
cherries, finely chopped
60 g (2¼ oz/½ cup) icing
(confectioners') sugar

135 g (4¾ oz/1½ cups)
desiccated coconut
125 ml (4 fl oz/½ cup)
condensed milk
60 g (2¼ oz) unsalted butter,
plus 25 g (1 oz) extra
50 g (1¾ oz) copha (white
vegetable shortening),
melted
150 g (5½ oz) dark chocolate,
chopped

Preheat the oven to 180°C (350°F/Gas 4). Lightly grease an 18 x 27 cm (7 x 10½ inch) rectangular shallow tin and line the base with baking paper, leaving the paper hanging over on the two long sides.

Sift the flour, cocoa and sugar into a bowl, add the butter and vanilla, and mix to form a dough. Turn onto a floured surface. Press together for 1 minute, then press into the base of the tin. Chill for 20 minutes. Cover with baking paper and baking beads and bake for 10–15 minutes. Remove the paper and beads and bake for 5 minutes. Cool. Combine the cherries, icing sugar and coconut. Stir in the condensed milk, butter and copha, then spread over the base. Chill for 30 minutes.

Melt the chocolate and butter in a heatproof bowl set over a saucepan of simmering water, making sure that the bowl does not touch the water. Pour over the cherry mixture, then chill until set.

MAKES 28 PIECES

Yoghurt cake with cinnamon lemon syrup

185 g (6½ oz) unsalted butter
250 g (9 oz/1 cup) caster
 (superfine) sugar
5 eggs, separated
250 g (9 oz/1 cup) Greek-style
 yoghurt
2 teaspoons grated lemon zest
½ teaspoon vanilla extract
280 g (10 oz/2¼ cups) plain
 (all-purpose) flour, sifted
2 teaspoons baking powder

½ teaspoon bicarbonate of soda
 (baking soda)
whipped cream, to serve

Syrup
250 g (9 oz/1 cup) caster
 (superfine) sugar
1 cinnamon stick
4 cm (1½ inch) strip lemon zest
1 tablespoon lemon juice

Preheat the oven to 180°C (350°F/Gas 4). Lightly grease a 10 x 20 cm (4 x 8 inch) loaf (bar) tin. Place the butter and sugar in a bowl and beat until light and creamy. Add the egg yolks gradually, beating well after each addition. Stir in the yoghurt, lemon zest and vanilla. Fold in the flour, baking powder and bicarbonate of soda.

Whisk the egg whites in a bowl until stiff peaks form and fold into the mixture. Spoon into the tin and bake for 50 minutes, or until a skewer inserted into the centre of the cake comes out clean. Leave in the tin for 10 minutes, then turn out onto a wire rack to cool completely.

Meanwhile, to make the syrup, place the sugar and cinnamon stick in a saucepan with 185 ml (6 fl oz/¾ cup) of water. Stir over medium heat until the sugar is dissolved. Bring to the boil, add the lemon zest and juice, then reduce the heat and simmer for 5–6 minutes. Strain. Pour the syrup over the cake. Cut into slices and serve with whipped cream.

SERVES 8–10

Baklava

560 g (1 lb 4 oz/2¼ cups) caster (superfine) sugar

1½ teaspoons lemon zest

90 g (3¼ oz/¼ cup) honey

3 tablespoons lemon juice

2 tablespoons orange blossom water

200 g (7 oz/2 cups) walnuts, finely chopped

200 g (7 oz/1⅓ cups) pistachio nuts, finely chopped

200 g (7 oz/1⅓ cups) almonds, finely chopped

2 tablespoons caster (superfine) sugar, extra

2 teaspoons ground cinnamon

375 g (13 oz) filo pastry

200 g (7 oz) unsalted butter, melted

Put the sugar, lemon zest and 375 ml (13 fl oz/1½ cups) of water in a pan and stir over high heat until the sugar dissolves, then boil for 5 minutes. Reduce the heat and simmer for 5 minutes. Add the honey, lemon juice and orange blossom water and cook for 2 minutes. Remove from the heat and refrigerate.

Preheat the oven to 170°C (325°F/Gas 3). Combine the nuts, extra sugar and cinnamon. Lightly grease a 27 x 30 cm (10½ x 12 inch) baking dish. Cover the base with a single layer of filo pastry and brush lightly with melted butter, folding in any overhanging edges. Continue to layer 10 more sheets of filo. Store the remaining filo under a damp tea towel (dish towel). Sprinkle half the nuts over the pastry and pat down. Repeat the layering and buttering of five more filo sheets, sprinkle with the rest of the nuts, then layer and butter the remaining filo, brushing the top with butter and pat down. Score into large diamonds. Pour any remaining butter over the top. Bake for 30 minutes, then reduce the heat to 150°C (300°F/Gas 2) and cook for 30 minutes. Immediately cut through the original diamond markings, then strain the syrup over the top. Refrigerate before serving.

MAKES 18 PIECES

Raspberry and coconut slice

280 g (10 oz/2¼ cups) plain (all-purpose) flour
3 tablespoons ground almonds
500 g (1 lb 2 oz/2 cups) caster (superfine) sugar
250 g (9 oz) unsalted butter, chilled
½ teaspoon ground nutmeg
½ teaspoon baking powder
4 eggs, at room temperature
1 teaspoon natural vanilla extract
1 tablespoon lemon juice
300 g (10½ oz/2½ cups) fresh or thawed frozen raspberries
90 g (3¼ oz/1 cup) desiccated coconut
icing (confectioners') sugar, to dust

Preheat the oven to 180°C (350°F/Gas 4). Lightly grease a 20 x 30 cm (8 x 12 inch) rectangular shallow tin and line the base with baking paper, leaving the paper hanging over on the two long sides.

Sift 220 g (7¾ oz/1¾ cups) of the flour into a bowl. Add the ground almonds and 125 g (4½ oz/½ cup) of the caster sugar and stir to combine. Rub the butter into the flour with your fingertips until it resembles fine breadcrumbs. Press the mixture into the tin and bake for 20–25 minutes, or until golden. Reduce the oven to 150°C (300°F/Gas 2).

Sift the nutmeg, baking powder and remaining flour onto a piece of baking paper. Beat the eggs, vanilla and remaining sugar using electric beaters until fluffy. Fold in the flour. Stir in the lemon juice, raspberries and coconut. Pour over the base and bake for 1 hour, or until golden. Chill in the tin, then cut into pieces. Dust with icing sugar.

MAKES 30 PIECES

index

First published in Australia in 2008 by Murdoch Books Pty Limited.
This edition published in 2009 by Bay Books, an imprint of Murdoch Books Pty Limited
This edition published 2009 for Index Books Ltd

Murdoch Books Australia
Pier 8/9, 23 Hickson Road
Millers Point NSW 2000
Phone: +61 (0) 2 8220 2000
Fax: +61 (0) 2 8220 2558
www.murdochbooks.com.au

Murdoch Books UK Limited
Erico House, 6th Floor
93–99 Upper Richmond Road,
Putney, London SW15 2TG
Phone: +44 (0) 20 8785 5995
Fax: +44 (0) 20 8785 5985
www.murdochbooks.co.uk

Chief Executive: Juliet Rogers
Publishing Director: Kay Scarlett

Design manager: Vivien Valk
Project manager and editor: Gordana Trifunovic
Design concept: Alex Frampton
Designer: Susanne Geppert
Production: Kita George
Cover photography: Tanya Zouev
Styling: Stephanie Souvlis
Introduction text: Leanne Kitchen
Recipes developed by the Murdoch Books Test Kitchen

Printed by 1010 Printing International Ltd in 2009.PRINTED IN CHINA.
Reprinted 2008.

ISBN 978 1 74196 5865

IMPORTANT: Those who might be at risk from the effects of salmonella poisoning (the
elderly, pregnant women, young children and those suffering from immune deficiency
diseases) should consult their doctor with any concerns about eating raw eggs.

CONVERSION GUIDE: You may find cooking times vary depending on the oven you
are using. For fan-forced ovens, as a general rule, set the oven temperature to 20°C (35°F)
lower than indicated in the recipe.